BLACK HOLOCAUST

The Paris Horror and a Legacy of Texas Terror

E. R. BILLS

Eakin Press
www.EakinPress.com

Front cover art (titled "Occidere") by Austin artist Paul Beck.

Copyright © 2015
By E.R. Bills
Published By Eakin Press
An Imprint of Wild Horse Media Group
P.O. Box 331779
Fort Worth, Texas 76163
1-817-344-7036
www.EakinPress.com
ALL RIGHTS RESERVED
1 2 3 4 5 6 7 8 9
ISBN-10: 1-68179-017-3
ISBN-13: 978-1-68179-017-6

ALL RIGHTS RESERVED. No part of this book may be reproduced in any form without written permission from the publisher, except for brief passages included in a review appearing in a newspaper or magazine.

Table of Contents

Preface v
Acknowledgments vii

Part I
1. The Paris Horror 1

Part II
2. 1861 34
3. 1863 36
4. 1867 38
5. 1876 40
6. 1890 42
7. 1891 44
8. 1892 47
9. 1895 49
10. 1901 54
11. 1902 62
12. 1905 67
13. 1908 78
14. 1909 82
15. 1910 86
16. 1912 92
17. 1915 95
18. 1916 104
19. 1919 108
20. 1920 113
21. 1921 118
22. 1922 121
23. 1924 132
24. 1930 134
25. 1933 142
26. Conclusion 148

Endnotes 159
Bibliography 166
Index 178
About the Author 188

Preface

hol·o·caust (häl'ə kôst') n. [ME. < OFr. holocauste < LL. (Ec.) holocaustum, a whole burnt offering < Gr. holokauston (neut. of holokaustos), burnt whole < holos, whole + kaustos, burnt] 1. an offering the whole of which is burned; burnt offering 2. great or total destruction of life, esp. by fire –the Holocaust [also h-] the systemic destruction of over six million European Jews by the Nazis before and during World War II.

Today the contemporary connotation or common perception of the term "holocaust" relates to the extermination/genocide of Jews by the Nazis before and during World War II. The original denotation or actual meaning of the term "holocaust," however, is burnt whole, a devastation of life by fire or a great or total destruction of life, especially by fire.

It can be argued that the Jews murdered by the Nazis were "burnt whole," but they were not burned to death or deprived of life by fire; they were killed by gas or other means before they were burned. Whether or not their burnings comprised an "offering" is a matter of philosophical interpretation.

In 1893—a half-century before "holocaust" came to signify the genocide perpetrated against the Jews—several holocausts occurred in the United States. A "Chicago Holocaust" resulted when twelve people accidentally burned to death in a building. A "frightful holocaust" occurred when seven men accidentally burned to death in a hotel in Beaver, Pennsylvania. A "sickening holocaust" took place when six people were accidentally burned alive at a lodging house in Burlington, Iowa. A "fearful holocaust" resulted when four people accidentally burned to death in a Cincinnati hotel. And a "terrible holocaust" occurred when a black man was tortured and burned at the stake in Paris, Texas.

In fact, the "Paris Horror" (as it was also called) would be referred to by Governor James Hogg, as the "holocaust at Paris" and it became a catalyst for a three-decade regimen of holocaust in Texas, intentionally perpetrated by whites against persons of color.

Burning a living, breathing human being at the stake is never simply a matter of murder or lynching. It's an act of terror, monstrosity and madness, and its political, societal and psychological repercussions are hardly quantifiable.

This book chronicles a period of holocaust and human cinder. If you're fragile—white or black—this is not a book for you.

E. R. Bills

Acknowledgements

Special thanks to the Texas State Library and Archive Commission, the Fort Worth Public Library, the Dallas Public Library, the University of North Texas Libraries, the Corsicana Public Library, the Hardin County Genealogical Society and Library and the Tyrell Historical Library.

I.

The Paris Horror

Masters of fiction have bent their energies to the utmost limits in efforts of word painting to show the extent to which cruelty of man may be carried, and still the horrors of man's inhumanity to man, as recorded in history, have not been reached by the most fertile imaginations. Accounts of Carthagenian cruelty, the horrors of the inquisitions of the Dark Ages, the fiendish torments inflicted upon prisoners by cruel savages, have curdled the blood of the reader for ages, but in no history, in no work of fiction, has such cruelty been reached as was witnessed at Paris, Texas, last week.

Dixon Evening Telegraph
February 4, 1893

The population of Paris, Texas in the 1890s was close to 10,000. It was a big town, but not so big that folks in the know weren't unaware of the troublesome sorts.

Henry Smith was an African American day-laborer in the community who liked to drink. When Smith was under the influence, he routinely had brushes with the law. Henry Vance was a white policeman who apparently had a penchant for beating suspects while they were in his custody.

Sometime around mid to late 1892 or early 1893, Smith's vice and Vance's penchant planted the seeds for a gruesome murder and a hellish lynching. Vance viciously beat or bullied Smith and Smith apparently devised a plan for vengeance. On the afternoon of Wednesday, January 24, 1893, Smith reportedly grabbed Vance's three-and-a-half-year-old daughter, Myrtle, and took her to the outskirts of town. Young Myrtle put up little resistance and Smith, initially at least, may not have had a clear notion as to what he would do with her.

Several witnesses, including Paris mayor Alexander Cate, claimed they saw Smith carrying Myrtle through town and thought little or nothing of it. African Americans in the South were still regularly employed as house servants, and the sight of a black man transporting Myrtle hardly registered except to one other little girl. As Smith allegedly passed by with Myrtle in his arms, the girl saw them and ran to her father, insisting he make Smith put Myrtle down. But the unidentified girl's father assumed Smith was collecting her for her folks.

As the cool January afternoon gave way to chilly evening, Myrtle didn't return home. By nightfall, the child was missed and the Vance family inquired after her, performing a cursory search. According to reports, Henry Vance was not overly troubled about Myrtle's whereabouts until he learned of Smith's possible involvement. And even then Vance's behavior was oddly subdued, as if he assumed Myrtle's disappearance was something of a prank rather than a matter of life or death.

Whatever the case, when the direction Smith reportedly carried Myrtle out of town was made known, Vance and a small search party examined the route and found nothing. Then—perhaps also curiously—the search was retired for the evening.

When Myrtle didn't return the following morning, a broader, organized investigation was conducted. Posses went out in every direction and one party went by Smith's estranged wife Sue's residence and spoke with her. Sue told investigators that Henry had spent the night out, returning home around daylight. She also said that when he came in he ordered her to fix him something to eat.

Sue had heard about the missing Vance girl and supposedly asked Smith about her, recommending that if he had grabbed her he should return her as soon as possible. His reported response was "Damn the white folks; I don't eat children."

Henry ate the breakfast Sue cooked and then left. The search efforts continued well into the day, unsuccessful until almost twenty-four hours after Myrtle's disappearance.

Around 3:30 p.m. gunshots rang out from the southeastern edge of Paris, signaling a break in the investigation. As members of the search effort converged on the spot where the gunfire originated, they were confronted by grim news.

In a densely forested area near the city dog pound, a pool of blood was discovered near a black jack tree. Next to the blood lay a worn, collapsed hat, a piece of cloth (thought to be a remnant of a child's underwear) and a pile of leaves that appeared to have borne weight through the cold night. The ground cover around the leaf pile was also disturbed, possibly evidencing a struggle.

Further scrutiny of the site revealed Myrtle Vance's mangled body approximately twenty feet from the pile of leaves that investigators surmised someone slept on. The corpse had been covered with leaves and concealed under briars and brush. When authorities extricated Myrtle's body from the bramble they noted bruising on the girl's face and neck and were shocked and appalled by what appeared to be the brutal violation and destruction of her vaginal area.

Depiction of Henry Smith's alleged victim, three-and-a-half-year-old Myrtle Vance. From *An Eye for An Eye or The Fiend and the Fagot: An Unvarnished Account of the Burning of Henry Smith at Paris, Texas, February 1, 1893, and the Reason he was Tortured* (1893).

An African American involved in the search reportedly identified the collapsed hat as belonging to Henry Smith and the piece of underwear discovered was confirmed to be part of the underclothing Myrtle had worn the day she disappeared. Local authorities transported Myrtle's body into town for official examination, and a description of her suspected assailant, Henry Smith, was widely circulated.

In the first *Dallas Morning News* coverage of the incident, titled "An Atrocity in Lamar" (on January 28, 1893), Smith was described as "a yellow, freckle-faced negro; tall, bulging forehead; coarse, open hair, not kinky; scar on right cheek and on side of head over right ear, thin beard on chin and thin mustache; large, wide-apart teeth. He wore a white-dotted bosom shirt, striped pants, coat and overcoat; blue overalls for drawers, boots with one heel gone, tops cut off; inside seam right boot tied with a string." The *Morning News* emphasized that Lamar County was being "ransacked by excited citizens and short mercy will be shown him [Smith] if caught."

In the *Fort Worth Gazette's* report of the same edition (titled "A Horrible Crime"), Henry Smith is described similarly, the *Gazette* clarifying that Smith was "about six feet high" and "thick-lipped" and notably expanding on the *Morning News'* prediction of "short mercy." The *Gazette* characterized Smith as a "black devil" responsible for the "most brutal crime that has ever disgraced Lamar County" and foretold that if apprehended and returned he would "expiate his crime at the hands of the people."[1]

Whether Smith's alleged intent was to kidnap Myrtle to scare Vance or rape and murder her to punish him is never sufficiently established. Whatever his rationale, Smith's vice played a role in the crime. It is unclear whether Smith had a bottle of liquor when he grabbed Myrtle, picked one up after he grabbed her or had one waiting in the woods where he allegedly took her; but at some point he got drunk. Eventually he passed out and Myrtle fell asleep near his person or, perhaps in the cold evening—as noted in Smith's probably coerced confession—even nestled innocently in his arms.

During the night, however, Smith awoke and, while still intoxicated, allegedly brutalized Myrtle and strangled her. Then, he evidently passed back out next to her body.

At approximately 5 a.m., before dawn, Smith re-awoke and, if his later reported confession can be believed, wasn't actually sure what had happened—but suspected what he had done. Then, indifferent (if his strange "I don't eat children" remark was indicative of his state of mind) or frightened and apprehensive, Smith began his flight.

According to Smith's reported confession, he went to the barn where he worked after he finished breakfast. He retrieved an old hat there (to replace the one he'd allegedly left at the crime scene) and then caught an eastbound Texas and Pacific freight train to Reno, informing the trainmen that he was traveling there to pick cotton for a man named George Reese. He loafed in Reno for an hour instead, and then walked to Blossom.

He arrived at Blossom at 3 p.m. and then hopped another freight train, stepping off at Detroit (Texas). In Detroit, he lingered around the station house, eventually chopping some wood to earn his supper. After eating, he walked to Bagwell, arriving around midnight.

While Smith was exiting Lamar County for Red River County, Myrtle Vance's autopsy was recorded by Paris City Health Officer J. B. Chapman, M. D., and W. S. Baldwin, M. D. Below is their sworn statement as to the findings:

> On the 26th day of January 1893, by request of A. Cate, mayor of Paris, and J. C. Hunt, Justice of the Peace Precinct #1, Lamar County, Texas, we examined the dead body of Myrtle Vance, aged about three years. We found the body in state of semi-rigidity and we based our opinion on this fact that death had occurred not more than six or eight hours previous. The chest, abdomen and lower extremities were covered with blood, bruises, under the angle of each jaw, giving evidence of an effort at strangulation, abrasion in front of the left ear. Found complete laceration of the perineum, extending an inch and a half up the rectum. The posterior part of the vagina ruptured, connecting abdominal cavity with vagina, parts terribly bruised and mutilated, unmistakable evidence of rape, hair from the monsveneris of the negro being found on the pudendum of the baby, held by the clotted blood. [2]

At Bagwell, Smith slept on the train platform until 4 a.m. and then caught a freight train to Clarksville, arriving on Saturday morning, January 28. There he milled around as inconspicuously as he could. By that point, however, the details of the crime and the initial description of his person had been bulletined to every telegraph officer in the region and talk of the horrifying murder of Myrtle Vance was on "every tongue." Back in Paris, Myrtle was buried after an emotional service and members of the local African American community authored resolutions denouncing Smith's crime and pledging to assist in his capture.

In Clarksville, Smith purchased a plate of food from a cook at a hotel and then jumped a freight train heading southeasterly. He met a man named Charley in a freight car and they stepped off together at De Kalb.

At De Kalb, Smith carried water for the proprietor of a local store

Portrait of Henry Vance. From *The Facts in the Case of the Horrible Murder of Little Myrtle Vance and its Fearful Expiation at Paris, Texas, February 1, 1893* (1893). Courtesy of Library of Congress.

in exchange for some bread and cheese. Charley had come from out west and carried a Winchester rifle. He was looking for a job and he and Smith left De Kalb at 8 p.m. on a freight headed to New Boston.

At New Boston, they exited the freight and walked to a tie camp en route to the Texas Central train junction. It was late when they arrived, but they stoked and maintained fires for the depot night operator in exchange for a warm spot to sleep inside. At 3 a.m., they caught a freight to Texarkana and arrived early on Sunday, January 29, remaining in the round house until morning. Then they took the Iron Mountain freight to Fulton, Arkansas.

In Fulton, Smith explored the town in search of some relatives and then he and Charley traveled to Sprendel's Mill on foot. Charley was able to get a job at the mill and Smith kept moving, at that point abandoning the railroad tracks.

Smith walked fourteen miles to Washington, Arkansas (farther northeast), arriving around midnight. He went straight to the train depot there and once again bartered with the night operator for shelter in exchange for fire duty. This time however, the night operator recognized Smith from his description in a recent dispatch and forwarded this information to Paris authorities that evening.

Smith left Washington on the morning of January 30 and walked six miles northeast to Ozan, where he chopped some wood in exchange for breakfast. Then he walked four more miles further northeast to a small community called Clow. On Tuesday, January 31st, he was apprehended there.

The entire time Henry Smith was making his way to Clow, Arkansas, law enforcement officials and opportunistic, would-be vigilantes in Texas were harassing an untold number of black men who fit his preliminary description. In an article titled "The Paris Horror" (January 29, 1893), the *Dallas Morning News* reported that potential suspects had been mistakenly confronted and/or jailed in Sherman, Sulphur Springs, Mount Vernon and Texarkana. And when a false report circulated in Sherman that Smith had already been captured and burned, a premature celebration broke out.

In Fort Worth a train station night watchman named Simmons saw an African American man step off an 8 p.m. Texas and Pacific freight train and decided it was Smith. He rushed to the union depot and contacted the police, but by the time he returned to the platform the suspect was gone. When the police arrived they decided that the suspect had crawled under some stock pens and fled into the stockyards. A squad of Fort Worth police officers subsequently combed the area and searched over twenty homes, but no evidence of Smith was found.

Paris officials sent investigators out in every direction and between the authorized investigators and the eager amateurs, tall, light-skinned, African American males became endangered citizens—then as now, racial profiling was a matter of course.

Some believed Smith was still in Paris and the *Morning News* reported that this suspicion had led "numerous irresponsible parties to do many indiscreet things, if not overt violations of the law."

On January 30, Mayor Cate addressed this problem, issuing the following proclamation:

> It having been brought to my notice repeatedly that unauthorized parties are annoying many of our white and black citizens by entering their premises with armed squads and searching there over and over again, I hereby warn all persons that such acts must be discontinued forthwith. The proper authorities are doing everything that can possible be done to bring Henry Smith to justice and no further searching of houses will be sanctioned unless the party is acting under the direct authority of an officer selected by the mayor or marshal.

This warning didn't dissuade the zealous sorts in Paris from assailing Smith's stepson, William Butler.

Though there was no evidence that Butler had in any way assisted Smith (or, for that matter, even had a close personal relationship with his stepfather), he was abruptly and continuously in danger. A preposterous rumor indicating that Butler, too, had decided to "revenge" himself upon a different police officer named Hamilton rapidly garnered credence and a lynching party of almost one hundred men mobilized. When Paris marshal Jim Shanklin became aware of the affair he relieved Hamilton of his badge and disbanded the small mob. By then Butler had already left town, but newspapers weren't optimistic about his future. The *Galveston Daily News* observed that he would probably be found "looking up a limb" by morning.

As the search for Smith continued, several investigators suspected he was en route to Oklahoma and/or the Indian territories because a significant number of African Americans who had once resided in Paris had relocated there. Also, sightings of Smith had been reported at an African American settlement on the Kiomatia River in northeast Red River County and in Antlers, Oklahoma.

Five days into the manhunt, Paris authorities conceded that the original, widely circulated description of Henry Smith had been inaccurate in some regards. Mayor Cate issued a revised description of the suspect and offered a reward:

> FIVE HUNDRED DOLLAR REWARD—Arrest Bob Dowery, alias Henry Smith, about 30 years old, six feet high, dark copper or ginger-bread color, loud spoken and stutters and stammers in speech, large gray eyes, large front teeth with space between them, small scar on one cheek near the ear, caused from a rising,[3] weighs about 170 pounds. He is wanted for the murder of a 3-year-old white child. When last seen he had on a light colored overcoat, dark striped pants, patched in the crotch, blue decking drawers, dark striped shirt, wore No. 10 boots, with one heel off and grain leather tops. Wears his hat pulled over the eyes. This above reward will be paid for the delivery of his body to the authorities of Paris, Tex.

Though the number of tips communicated in regards to Smith's whereabouts is unknown, the city of Paris received dozens of letters and telegrams from individuals imploring city officials to inform them when Smith was apprehended so they could make arrangements to attend his much-anticipated, summary execution. Most area residents already assumed Smith's punishment would be a public burning at the stake, and this assumption was not unreasonable. For crimes that saw white men imprisoned or hanged after a trial or infrequently hanged by a lynch-mob, black men regularly faced a lynch-mob's noose or torch without a trial. In fact, less than a year prior, an estimated 1,000 Texarkana citizens had burned an African American man named Ed Coy at the stake for allegedly "ravishing" a white woman.

For the first four days of the search, law enforcement personnel, deputized assistants, keen vigilantes and self-appointed bounty hunters combed every inch of northeast Texas with very little luck, chasing down rumors, employing hounds and interrogating every lone black man they encountered who fit (or approached fitting) one of the descriptions. In the end, none of them got their man, but they did get other men that they mistakenly presumed to be Smith.

On the evening of January 30, approximately seven miles west of Clarksville, a search party surrounded the house of a local African American named Clem Brooks. No doubt aware of the dangers of being a black man in the midst of the Henry Smith manhunt (and the corollary vigilante-style proceedings occurring in the region) Brooks grew frightened and ran. The search party fired on him, one shot entering his back and another breaking his leg above the knee. The wounds were probably fatal, but there was no evidence his attackers faced any consequences for their error.

On January 31—the same day Smith was captured—another African American man living near Bagwell Station in Red River County was followed to his home and ordered by an unofficial posse to come out and identify himself. He, like Brooks, did not trust his summoners and decided to run. The posse opened fire and he was seriously (if not mortally) wounded and, like Brooks, promptly identified as someone other than Smith. Once again, however, there was no evidence his attackers faced any consequences for their error.

In addition to these homicidal blunders and during the same time frame that Smith was being reported captured without a struggle and alive, he was also reported captured after a gunfight and suffering from four gunshot wounds after refusing to surrender to a man named G. M. Crook.[4] It is unlikely that Brooks and the African American shot near Bagwell Station were the only black men gunned down during the manhunt.

The actual arrest of Henry Smith was fairly uneventful. After the night operator in Washington, Arkansas (among others) contacted Paris officials and reported Smith's presence in the area firsthand, municipal leaders sent Lamar County Attorney B. B. Sturgeon, County Tax Collector B. Walters and two African American citizens, Naby Robertson and Gilbert Owens, who knew Smith on sight. When the Paris contingent arrived in the area, they were joined by local, Hempstead County (Arkansas) personnel, including H. B. Holman, J. L. White, James Robinson and James T. Hicks. The group split up and Holman, White, Robinson, Hicks and Robertson headed to Ozan to investigate reports that Smith had been spotted in the community.

From Ozan they visited Clow and were informed that a man matching the suspect's description had recently arrived there and at that moment was thought to be partaking of a local spring. The Holman search party headed for the spring and discovered Smith there on his hands and knees having a drink. When Smith finished and stood up, the five searcher's guns were trained on him and he surrendered immediately.

Smith seemed surprised as the small band handcuffed and arrested him, claiming that he had done nothing wrong. The party turned back towards Ozan and Smith repeatedly reiterated his innocence.

When quizzed about his abrupt departure from Paris, Smith suggested it was a whim that he acted on while drunk. As members of the party pressed him to confess his crime, he told them he had no idea what they were talking about.

In Ozan, Hicks telegrammed Mayor Cate:

> We have captured Henry Smith. Will leave Hope at 6:50 a.m. tomorrow.

In Washington, B. B. Sturgeon sent a separate, Paris delegation telegram to Cate:

> Have got the negro. Will reach Paris at 12:06. Be prepared to protect us.

Confirmations made, the party was now—as the last line of Sturgeon's telegram suggests—concerned with the level of mob interest and interference they might face during their return trip to Lamar County.

Hicks and Sturgeon and their men got Smith to Hope early enough for them to take a train to Texarkana, but the possibility of a layover there gave them all pause. As previously noted, an African American man named Coy had been lynched in Texarkana less than a year before and, by all indications, elements of the community there were spoiling for a sequel. Reports suggested that a thousand men had met Smith and the civic Arkansas and Texas contingents at the train depot in Hope; they knew the numbers in Texarkana would be higher. They decided to spend the night in Hope.

Henry Smith at the Union Depot in Paris, Texas. His executioner, Henry Vance, is standing immediately left. *Frank Hudson, ca. 1900. International Center of Photography, Gift of Daniel Cowin, 1990.*

The crime committed against Myrtle Vance had generated a wave of outrage and indignation throughout the entire region and the resultant fervor showed no sign of abating. Once word spread that Smith was in custody and en route to Paris, huge throngs of the appalled, curious and vengeful would mass at stops along the way.

Realizing this, Mayor Cate and other Paris leaders decided not to leave anything to chance. They sent an additional fifty armed men (hundreds volunteered) on a special train to Texarkana to take control of Smith and ensure his arrival in Paris.

The next morning, February 1, Sturgeon and the armed escort transported Smith from Hope to Texarkana on a Texas and Pacific train. Swarms of people (estimated to number in the thousands) greeted the group at the Texarkana depot and the unruly multitude demanded to see Smith. Smith's captors obliged the mob, but the throng's glimpse was reportedly cut short when one of the onlookers drew a pistol and had to be subdued.

Every stop the rest of the way was virtually a reoccurrence of the spectacle at Texarkana. Huge crowds scrambled to get a look at Smith (at one station an onlooker took a swipe at him when he stuck his head out a window) and large numbers of folks attempted to board the train to Paris to see his execution. Most latecomers were turned away because there was no room.

Smith reportedly maintained his innocence until the train reached De Kalb. When his captors explained that they were sure of his guilt and that he was scheduled to be burned at the stake, Smith supposedly admitted the crime but insisted he had been drunk and didn't recall much of it. He subsequently implored one of his captors to save him, but was told that there was nothing that could be done.

After contemplating the planned manner of his death, Smith begged to be shot but was petrified by the thought of being shot by Vance. He requested an execution by Marshal Shanklin or Mayor Cate. When Smith's captor's reiterated what the citizens of Paris had in store for him, he shuddered and asked to be permitted to kill himself. When his entreaties were ignored, Smith became "a picture of terror and despair."

On January 31, the city of Paris hadn't just sent an armed escort to Texarkana to bring Henry Smith back; they had also collectively and definitively determined Smith's sentence and punishment.

Smith's guilt had long been established in the public mind and Parisians saw no need for the normal, constitutionally mandated rights of due process or a trial hearing. It was generally agreed upon that Smith would be ceremoniously tortured by members of the victim's family and then burned at the stake. And it was also determined that the procedure should not be accomplished by an unruly, disorganized mob somewhere out in the backwoods. Leading Paris officials would oversee it and construct proper staging for the solemn process in or near the community:

> Lumber was taken far out on an open prairie southeast of the T. & P. depot, in full view of the town and the railroad, and there a scaffold ten feet high was firmly erected, with every appliance necessary for the final act in the tragedy. When the morning of February 1st broke beautifully upon the face of nature, the monstrous engine... appeared upon the landscape to meet the rising sun. It rose up like a grim specter and bore the verdict of a united

people upon its ominous front in the one word "Justice!" The crime was beyond description in words borne in even our prolific language. Our statute books held, in all their pages of fact and precedent, no law worthy to mete out justice in such a case; and now the morning of February 1st silently revealed the solution of the problem, and all the people responded, "Amen!"[5]

As *Paris Daily News* columnist Alexander Neville put it, "the people felt a crime that had never been contemplated by the law had been committed and they made a law to fit it as nearly as possible." Actually, the citizens hadn't crafted a law; they simply crafted a punishment. And it quickly became the event of the season.

The Paris that Henry Smith was returning to was hellishly festive. Folks from Dallas, Fort Worth, Sherman, Denison, Bonham, Texarkana and southern Arkansas were pouring into the city to witness the spectacle as rapidly as the supplemented train service could deliver them. They wanted to see the "loathsome freight of incarnate fiendishness" arrive. They wanted to be able to say "I was there" when the "beast" was burned. Civic duty rarely afforded a community as much publicity and anticipation as the public execu-

The scaffold of "Justice."
From *The Facts in the Case of the Horrible Murder of Little Myrtle Vance and its Fearful Expiation at Paris, Texas, February 1, 1893* (1893). *Courtesy of Library of Congress.*

tion of Henry Smith would; it was clear that the town and the burgeoning crowd waited with baited breath for the man (or monster) of the hour. Many shops and businesses closed for the event and the execution's chief witnesses, Mayor Cate, shuttered all the saloons and gave schoolchildren the day off.

The only serious attempt to dampen the proceedings came from Governor James Hogg. After word reached Austin that Henry Smith had been captured and was being transported back to Paris, Governor Hogg sent two early telegrams.

> Austin, Tex., Feb. 1. —*To the County Attorney. Paris: Your conduct in having Smith arrested deserves special commendation. See that he has a fair trial in the courts, to the end that he may be legally punished.* –J. S. Hogg.

> Austin, Tex., Feb. 1. —*To the Sheriffs of Lamar and Bowie counties: Use all lawful means to see that Henry Smith is protected from mob violence and is brought to trial for his crime before the lawful authorities. Mobs must not be permitted to try prisoners in Texas.* –J. S. Hogg.

Governor Hogg received quick responses:

> Paris, Tex., Feb. 1. —*To Governor Hogg: I am helpless; have no support.* –D. S. Hammond, Sheriff.

> Paris, Tex., Feb. 1. —*To Governor Hogg: Officers are helpless; the enraged public stands waiting for the prisoner, who is expected at 1 o'clock.* –A. McCuistion, Assistant County Attorney.

Governor Hogg replied:

> Austin, Tex., Feb. 1.—*To the Sheriff of Lamar County: If you need help call for it. By all means protect the majesty of the law and the honor of Texas and your people from committing murder.* –J. S. Hogg.

> Austin, Tex., Feb. 1.—*To the assistant county attorney of Lamar County: Wire those in charge of the prisoner not to bring him to Paris. Guard him safely and use every effort to prevent the mob from reaching him.* –J. S. Hogg.

Governor Hogg's supplications came too late. He received one more telegram before the execution:

> Paris, Tex., Feb. 1.—*To Governor J. S. Hogg: Henry Smith has arrived and is in charge of 5,000 to 10,000 enraged citizens. I am utterly helpless to protect him.* –D. S. Hammond, Sheriff.

When the train carrying Henry Smith arrived, an anxious mob

of thousands waited at the depot. As Smith's captors presented him on the platform in Paris, he gazed at the hostile public and collapsed pitifully to the platform surface. His captors seized him under his arms and raised him to a standing position.

In an added bit of theatre, Parisian ingenuity was not limited to the grim scaffold of "Justice" on the adjacent prairie. Citizens had also decked a freight-float (hitched to four mules) with an elevated chair on which Smith could be paraded around the downtown on while en route to the scaffold. Several armed men road alongside the float on horseback as guards. Smith was securely bound to the elevated perch and city officials attempted to commence the procession, but the deranged cavalcade was thwarted by the sheer number of onlookers.

Throughout the morning of Wednesday, February 1, the temperature in Lamar County grew increasingly frigid. As officials spent the better part of an hour clearing a path for the morbid cavalcade, it began to rain. As the rain settled on hats, umbrellas and rooftops, it froze and steam rose from the mules that dragged the freight-float. Smith sat atop the procession, bareheaded and horrified. Every vantage point was filled with unfriendly glares and the only sounds besides the mule and horse hooves and the light chatter of human teeth was Smith's rueful, stammering entreaties to be shot. The mob was unmoved.

The crowd was filled with armed men, but bullets, like the noose, had been ruled too merciful for Smith. The citizens of Paris had made the calculation that Smith's introduction to hellfire and damnation couldn't wait for an afterlife—he would face it then, at their hands.

The cavalcade wound its way around the town square and then turned toward the scaffold of "Justice." As the freight-float passed, the mob fell in behind and followed it into the open prairie, maneuvering for positions that afforded optimal viewing. Some say the onlookers numbered ten thousand; others reported fifteen thousand. As the freight-float reached the scaffold, twenty to thirty thousand eyes watched city officials assist Smith in his shaky ascent of the scaffold stairs in the drizzle and freezing rain.

What happened next wrote itself. As the *Galveston Daily News*

The beginning of Henry Smith's torture.
From *The Facts in the Case of the Horrible Murder of Little Myrtle Vance and its Fearful Expiation at Paris, Texas, February 1, 1893* (1893). Courtesy of Library of Congress.

put it, no effort was "made to exaggerate it in any of the reports. It could not be exaggerated."

Henry Smith was securely bound and fastened with ropes to the large wooden stake that rose up through the ten-foot platform of the scaffold of "Justice." As participants finished the ropes, Henry Vance addressed the crowd, detailing the devastating sense of loss and grief he had felt after and since the horrifying murder of Myrtle and sharing the depth of his family's pain and anguish.[6] Vance was subsequently joined by his twelve-year-old son, Beuford,[7] and one of his brother-in-laws. The trio waited patiently while various local politicians and dignitaries gave speeches and made pronouncements, and then they and a couple of "torture" attendants were left alone on the scaffold with Smith.

At this point, Smith reportedly confessed again, and his statement was relayed to the crowd by those on the platform. Then the attendants removed Smith's shoes and pulled out pocket knives, cutting away his jacket and/or shirt, leaving his torso bare. As they dropped pieces of his clothing to the crowd below (which many greedily gathered as mementoes), tinner's furnaces containing pre-heated irons were placed on the scaffold and Smith's macabre sentence commenced.

Taking turns, Vance, his son Beuford and Vance's brother-in-law removed red-hot irons from the tinner's furnaces and laid them into Smith's flesh, starting at the soles of his feet. As the glowing metal met Smith's skin he howled, but his wails were drowned out by hoots and hollers from the crowd.

After Smith's feet, his torturers progressed upward to his calves and then his thighs, burning him through his britches. Every baleful moan and wail was met with cheers; every quiver and contortion was met with scoffs and approbation. Used, flesh-matted irons were replaced in the tinner's furnaces, and blazing, freshly heated irons were re-employed. And the torturers grew more proficient as they went.

Initially, the Vance clan just poked Smith or laid an iron on his britches until it burned through and seared his hide. When they made it to Smith's bare back and abdomen, however, they began to roll the red hot irons, ensuring the most efficient use of the glowing metal surfaces and delivering the maximum level of pain and agony. The effectiveness of this tactic, burning and pealing Smith's skin away from his torso in the frigid air, delighted the mob and kept them maniacally invested. The gory montage of the deed and the stench of scorched flesh gave them no pause whatsoever—this was what they had come to see.

By the time the Vance avengers applied the red-hot irons to Smith's arms and shoulders, he was less responsive, the physical excruciation of the epidermal trauma presumably leading to a flood of endorphins, etc., sparing him some of the pain. That may have been why Vance abandoned the epidermal onslaught.

A public punishment as novel and gruesome as Smith's could not end in a whimper or faint, especially from the object of the torment. For the climax of the tribulation, then, the Vance clan poked fiery, red-hot irons into Smith's eye sockets, one after another, vaporizing his eyeballs and jogging him from a temporarily merciful state of semi-consciousness. Sightless and quavering (and probably semi-rational), Smith never saw the final red-hot poker before it was shoved down his mouth and throat, and probably wasn't sure of what was happening as his tongue and upper esophageal lining were seared away.

Illustration depicting a tortured Henry Smith (head collapsed back) on the scaffold just before the kindling beneath it is lit. *Fort Worth Gazette*, 1893.

For fifty minutes, the Vance clan had retrieved, replaced and re-retrieved red-hot irons from the tinner's furnaces and charred Smith's feet, legs, arms, back and abdomen, eliciting blood-curdling shrieks and groans from the sufferer, which in turn were answered by spirited cheers and encouragement from onlookers. Smith was now a blind, muted ligament of scorched human flesh, his head lowered, his chin resting on his chest. He hardly responded when his executioners heaped cottonseed hulls at his feet and poured kerosene over his person. But when the kerosene was lit and the rising fire briefly engulfed him in a cocoon of blue flame, Smith's head rose and his eyeless, speechless visage was cast skyward. What had been his mouth emitted a soundless lament and a billow of smoke "that looked like steam from an escape line." His silent cry was met by shouts and laughter.

Then, in an unforeseen twist, the fire burned away Smith's binds

Illustration depicting Henry Smith on the scaffold as it is engulfed in flames. *Fort Worth Gazette*, 1893.

and he slid off the burning scaffold and slipped to the earth. His smoldering body was motionless, but spectators pushed it back into the fire anyway.

Miraculously—and no doubt surreally—what was left of Smith writhed and squirmed free of the flames, shocking onlookers. His pants had been burned away and his body was broiled coal black. There was nothing left of his hands and feet except limbs of fire-melded sinew and bone, and yet he twisted and squirmed, perhaps only instinctively or reflexively, but he still struggled—which seemed impossible.

Members of the mob kicked or pushed him back into the flames and he rolled out again. This time, however, onlookers place a rope around his neck and re-subjected him to the conflagration, restricting him to the hellish pyre until his life and grotesque exertions were completely extinguished.

When the flames and coals died down, memento seekers raked the ashes, fighting over teeth and bits of bone. As the "fearful expiation" ended and the crowd dispersed, McCuistion wired Hogg:

> Paris, Tex., Feb. 1.—*To Governor J. S. Hogg: All is over. Death by hot iron torture. A diabolical affair.* –E. A. McCuistion, Assistant County Attorney.

Hogg replied pointedly:

> Austin, Tex., Feb. 1.—*To E. A. McCuistion, Paris: Do your whole duty and prosecute every person engaged in the reported lynching of one Henry Smith at Paris. By all means preserve the names of the offenders and witnesses, to the end that the guilty parties may be prosecuted.* –J. S. Hogg.

On February 2 the *Galveston Daily News* noted that the torture and immolation of Henry Smith had "burnt and seared itself into every mind so vividly that it stands before all who gazed upon it as distinctly now as when they witnessed it." A headline in the *New York Times* dolefully lamented "Another Negro Burned."[8]

The *Dallas Morning News* headline called the lynching the "Horror of Horrors," a subhead suggesting that it harked back to the final days of the Roman Empire. The *Marshall Evening Messenger* headlines said "It Reads Like A Chapter in Medieval History" and "The Scene Appalling As He Rubbed His Eyeless Sockets With The Stumps of His Arms and In Shocked Agony." And the *Boston Post* front page was unequivocal. It deemed Smith's execution "White Savagery" and claimed "Civilization Seemingly a Failure in Texas."

But for every newspaper that decried the act, there were counterparts who condoned if not commended it. A *Boston Daily Globe* front page included a headline that simply read "Burned At Stake"

View of the crowd witnessing the carnival-atmosphere lynching of Henry Smith. From *The Facts in the Case of the Horrible Murder of Little Myrtle Vance and its Fearful Expiation at Paris, Texas, February 1, 1893* (1893). Courtesy of Library of Congress.

and the sub-heads "Terrible Punishment for Negro Murderer" and "Best Citizens of Paris, Tex., Aid in the Affair." The *Arizona Republican* quaintly announced a "Death by Fire." The headline of Missouri's *Springfield Leader* reported "Myrtle Vance Avenged." The *Los Angeles Herald* headline read "Burned at the Stake" with the subhead "Fearful Vengeance Wreaked on Colored Fiend." And the *Fort Worth Gazette* headline was plainly exculpatory. It read "Branded, Blistered, Burned," sub-heading "Roasted, was the Animal Form of Rapist-Murderer-Savage-Fiendish Negro, Henry Smith," and "Caucasian Vengeance for African Barbarity."

To most Texans and many Americans, the torture and burning of Henry Smith was justice. But to some folks, including Governor James Hogg, it clearly was not. And he dispatched two telegrams demanding the enforcement of his position:

> Austin, Tex., Feb. 2.—*To the Sheriff of Lamar County Paris, Tex.: Discharge your sworn duty as an officer of the state faithfully and fearlessly. Promptly make complaint before the proper officers against every person known to have been engaged in the lynching of the negro Henry Smith at Paris yesterday, and report the names of all the witnesses to the district and county attorney, to the end that all the*

guilty persons may be effectively prosecuted. –J. S. Hogg, Governor of Texas.

Austin, Tex., Feb. 2.—*N. P. Doak, District Attorney, Clarksville, Tex.: In the lynching of negro Henry Smith in Paris on yesterday the laws of the state have been openly defied. Every good citizen is interested in maintaining and enforcing the laws of the land. Either law and order or anarchy must prevail, and there can be no compromise on middle ground. Mob law in Texas must be stamped out. It is believed and expected that you will promptly, diligently and persistently inquire into and ascertain who are the guilty parties and faithfully and fearlessly prosecute them. Any assistance needed will be promptly rendered.* –J. S. Hogg, Governor of Texas.

Despite additional runs and special editions, the local and state reporting of Henry Smith's torture and incineration sold newspapers out as fast as they could be printed. And after the initial story was told, publishers followed up with "aftermath" reporting, responses to the lynching and a record of Governor Hogg's telegrams before and after the incident.

Several newspapers observed the general sense of satisfaction and quietude after the lynching. The February 3 edition of the *Fort Worth Gazette* ran a headline proclaiming that "It Was Just" because the rape and murder of Myrtle Vance had been "A Crime Above Law." The same edition of the *New York Times* included a front page headline noting "Paris Citizens Proud of It," reporting that "all who participated in the torture of the negro Smith yesterday boldly proclaimed today the part they took in the affair and said they had no fear of arrest." And the collective self-righteousness extended well beyond the boundaries of Lamar County. Several newspapers published affirmations of the deed.

The February 2 edition of the *Paris Daily News* revealed that reports of Smith's lynching were endorsed by the people of Cleburne, "received with shouts of joy" in Sulphur Springs ("in commendation of the heroic efforts to suppress this class of diabolical outlaws"), "generally approved by all classes" of citizens in Texarkana and met with "rejoices" in Marshall. The *Galveston Daily News* reported that Smith's capture had brought a "sigh of relief" to the population of Abilene and that the majority of the citizens in Denison and Victoria approved of the burning of Smith.

The *Dallas Times-Herald* wrote that "the people of Paris and La-

New York Herald telegram requesting a 500-word opinion on the Henry Smith lynching from Governor James Hogg. *Courtesy of Texas State Library and Archive Commission.*

mar County had done well" and that the "death of the fiendish murderer and raper of little four-year-old Myrtle Vance was received everywhere with joy and satisfaction."

The *Austin Statesman* proclaimed that "every true man in the South would rather die than yield one iota of his right to visit dire and terrible vengeance upon the brute or brutes who desecrate and humiliate the purity of Southern homes" and said to let the Smith lynching be "a lesson to the brutes, white or black, who touch with unhallowed hand the women of the country."

Several notable, local citizens went on record. J. C. Hodges, a prominent Paris attorney said "Like all men of my profession I have the deepest reverence for the law and have all my life been a steadfast opponent of lynch law, and am yet, but this matter was one that rose higher than law." Denison doctor Julian C. Field starkly quipped that Smith would "hardly do such a thing again" and that it was "a good example."

One successful Denison merchant (who asked not to be identified) went a step further: "We are exceedingly tired of upholding law in such cases when law does not uphold or protect us. Such devils fly to the courts and jails for refuge. Last year in Grayson County there were about thirty cold blooded murders, some of them of the most cruel and diabolical nature, and we have had only one hanging to offset the entire list. Smith deserved all the punishment he got and if the dose was given to a few white men our state would be all the better off."

Other citizens from around the country also weighed in. In a February 3 letter to Henry Vance, Missouri resident Charles Balmer (of the Balmer and Weber Music House Company in St. Louis) sent his "greatest praise" for "dealing so summarily with the villainous brute" and lamented the fact his community didn't have citizens like Vance there "to deal with our jail full of criminals and murderers who live on the labors of us tax payers and who are continually being set free by some red tape of the law."

The record of Governor Hogg's telegrams was widely published—and just as widely dismissed.

Some critics insisted that Hogg's denunciation and sudden prosecutorial urgency in regards to what had transpired was simply for show and little more than an obligatory "bluff,"[9] and that he could do little else in the wake of the matter. Others pointed out that if Hogg had acted more quickly, instructing Arkansas governor William Meade Fishback to prevent the Arkansas law enforcement personnel from handing Smith over to the Paris contingent (especially as the Paris concern was without warrant or other official directive), he could have mustered and dispatched a large Texas force to secure Smith and deliver him to the proper, reinforced authorities.

The lynching became a topic of newspaper comment sections and editorial pages around the country. The *Chicago Daily Globe* was disbelieving:

> If the story of the torture and the burning of Henry Smith is not a fake, which the Daily Globe believes it to be, the people of Paris, Tex., should move en masse to Dahomey[10] or to the beautiful Congo basin... Before becoming too indignant it will be well to wait for a confirmation of the amazing story.

The *Lenoir Topic* in North Carolina was condemnatory:

> If it was not wrong for a Christian to torture the negro, then the Paris multitude was right to stand by and allow the poor,

demented parent of the little girl to follow the instincts of the vengeful passions that were aroused by his nature. If it was an unchristian act, then the Paris people are much more to be condemned than the poor man who is scarcely to be held accountable for what he did in the crazed condition of his mind. It is not even a question of the right or wrong of lynch law. The negro should have been shot or hung at once. It is not a question of whether the depraved outlaw deserved more or less punishment. It is simply a question of humanity—a question of whether civilization should practice the revolting crimes of barbarism.

The *Los Angeles Herald* pointed out that "the old theological tenets held that just such tortures as Smith was made to endure are dealt out to the sinner through all eternity, and by the express will of Almighty God himself"—as if there was nothing wrong with the citizens of Paris giving Smith a preview of Hell before he was presumably sent there. The *Indianapolis Sentinel* said that it seemed "incredible that in this country and this age such a barbarous and inhuman spectacle could be enacted" and inferred that it was a lapse that lowered the "moral tone" of the entire state.

The *San Antonio Express* published an emotional affirmation:

> The blood of the innocent has not cried to heaven in vain for vengeance. The black beast that ravished the white babe at Paris, Texas, has paid the penalty of his accursed crime—has perished at the stake, has passed through hell of fire upon earth to the hotter flames of an eternal Hades hereafter.
>
> The constitution was set aside, the laws suspended, the car of civilization rolled back a thousand years. Goaded to madness by a deed demonic, a proud and prosperous people forgot the precepts of God, the laws of man and revolted in a moment to a state of savagery, reveled in cruelty that might well make devils blush...
>
> The world will judge the people of Paris; but ere it do so let it place the dead babe beside the charred remains of the demon who caused her death. Before it allows the shrieks of the ravisher on his funeral pyre to attune its heart to pity, let it hearken to the screams of his little victim in the dead of the night, in that lonely wood as she cried to parents who were powerless to protect.
>
> Sorrowful as it is to see a people's passion over-ride the law, evil as the precedent may be, we can not wish the deed undone. The Paris episode will strike a healthy terror to the cowardly

hearts of beasts, both white and black, that prey on innocence—that despoil both the cradle and the grave to feed lust's unholy fires.

The *Nebraska State Journal's* criticism was pointed:

> The Texans can give the Comanches and the Apaches some points on the art of diabolical torture that would be considered valuable by those savages. It is true that the wretch they roasted after searing his entire body with red hot irons, was as barbarous as themselves, but he lacked the hereditary civilization and culture of the Caucasian, and should have been readily accorded a superiority in fiendishness over his betters. The spectacle so much enjoyed of the slow burning of the brutal negro makes civilization sick at the stomach.

Less philosophically, the *St. Louis Republic* bluntly (and quite condescendingly in regards to the victim) strafed the perpetrators:

> By their appalling crimes of yesterday the people of Paris, Texas, degraded themselves to the level of the brute they tortured, and fixed upon their community a stigma which it will take years of the law-abiding life of a civilized people to efface. They have avenged a fiendish crime with a crime as fiendish, and the more inexcusable because it was a crime not of a bestial negro but of citizens who no doubt pride themselves on their superior civilization and enlightenment.

And Pennsylvania's *Canonsburg Weekly Notes* posited a proactive proposal:

> That class of Americans who are hip, hip, hurrahing for more territory; who want Canada annexed this year, Mawian islands purchased the next, and South Africa the year after, it strikes us havn't got as much sense as they ought to have or as they might have, if they would keep quiet a little while and give their "think shop" a chance to do some work. We have enough of territory, more than we have stocked with the right kind of people. There is only one condition on which we should be willing to have the country invest in more territory, viz.: If an island of sufficient size could be had at a reasonable figure, take it, and as soon as the papers are signed, sealed and delivered, gather the brutes who burned the negro at Paris, Texas, last week, together with their apologists and defenders. . . and ship them all to it, and then declare an everlasting quarantine against the island. We would favor a purchase for this purpose but for no other.

On February 4, United States Senator George Frisbie Hoar[11] brought the issue of lynching in the South to the floor of the Senate, presenting a petition protesting the crime collected and signed by concerned African Americans in Washington, D. C. Senator Hoar called upon his colleagues to advise the Senate Judiciary Committee to grant a hearing of the petition "in respect to the lawless outrages committed in some of the southern states upon persons accused of crime, but who are denied the ordinary means of establishing their innocence by due process of law."

Hoar's request was never taken up in earnest, but discussion and debate in regards to the torture and open-air incineration of Henry Smith never waned the week following the lynching, and on Monday, February 6, Governor Hogg surprised his doubters and incensed his critics by vigorously reiterating his stance in an official letter to the Texas Legislature:

The headstone for the grave of Myrtle Vance. The monument was paid for donations raised by local Paris children and their families. *Author's collection.*

> It becomes my painful duty to emphasize to you the necessity of taking some steps to prevent mob violence in Texas. The recent terrible holocaust at Paris is but an illustration to what extent the mob spirit will go when the laws are inadequate to check it. While the victim of that affair was guilty of an atrocious, barbarous crime, appalling to contemplate, for which he was certain of full punishment under the Constitution and laws of our State, civilization stands as a helpless witness to the most revolting execution of the age, in which large numbers of citizens openly, in broad day, publicly became murderers by methods shameful to

humanity.

    Brushing away all sentiment, which should never accompany punishment for crime, the public murder committed at Paris is a disgrace to this state. Its atrocity, inhumanity and sickening effect upon the people at large cannot be obscured by reference to the savage act of the culprit himself in brutally taking the life of an innocent child. For his deed the death penalty awaited him under the law. The imputation that he could not have been legally executed in any court in this State is a slander upon the integrity of every citizen. To contend that his executioners, who publicly murdered him, can either be indicted or tried in the county where the crime was committed is a pretense and a mockery. So, the condition exists in our State that while one man may be convicted for murder, a hundred men who publicly commit murder cannot be. The laws, therefore, without further legislation, may be held in defiance in any community where the forces are strong enough to overawe the local officers and set aside the legal machinery of justice. Our constitution is not so hide bound that this condition must continue.

Hogg's letter to the legislature went on to outline suggestions that would specifically criminalize and punish citizens and communities involved in lynchings and the message was conveyed to the public in its entirety in newspapers on February 7. Later, the same day, the *Paris Daily News* contacted Henry Smith's wife, Sue, to secure a statement disparaging Smith because "a number of citizens desired that the facts might be got and placed before the public in order that those people who are making a martyr of him and saying that the citizens of Paris are more degraded than he, may see how depraved a brute he was." Mrs. Smith was transported to the office of a notary public named J. R. G. Long and signed off on the following statement:

> I am the widow of the late Henry Smith, who was executed on the first day of February, 1893, at Paris, Texas, for the murder of little Myrtle Vance; I lived with Henry Smith for one and one-half years as his wife; my daughter, Leila, 8 years old, also lived with us; as many as a dozen times said Henry Smith attempted (after we had all retired for the night) to ravish and have carnal intercourse with my daughter and his step-daughter, and was only prevented from accomplishing his fiendish purpose by my interference, and on more than one occasion inflicted serious bodily injury upon me for my interference; on account of said

> Smith's persistent efforts and attempts to ravish and ruin my little 8-year-old daughter, Leila, I was forced to keep her away from home and out of his reach and presence; we were married about seven years ago, and on account of his brutal nature and cruel treatment of my little daughter I was forced to separate from him, and was not living with him at the time of the occurrence for which he was executed.

Sue Smith signed the document with an "X" and Long notarized it. As Sue was likely illiterate, the statement was written utilizing a level of diction that was not hers and possibly beyond her comprehension. The information contained therein may have been factual, but considering the obvious filter, the testimony may have been led and orchestrated and the interpretation presented in such a way that was most useful to Parisian narrative of the suspect and the events leading up to the lynching.

On February 8, the day after Sue's statement—and the day it appeared in the *Paris Daily News*—William Butler, Henry Smith's stepson, was found "hanging to a limb and riddled with bullets" along Hickory Creek five miles southeast of Paris. Butler's death was generally accepted as the conclusion of unfinished business (referred to in one newspaper as "A Sequel to the Paris Lynching") and never seriously investigated or prosecuted. The sudden "deposition" of Sue Smith and subsequent lynching of Butler certainly and not-so-coincidentally tidied up any loose ends in the accusation against and grotesque execution of Henry Smith and may have eliminated any possible conflicting evidence or testimony that might have sullied the official account of the affair; and this was especially convenient and timely considering Governor Hogg's emphatic November 6 reiteration of his commitment to justice in such cases.

On the day William Butler's lynched corpse was discovered, responses to Hogg's letter to the Texas Legislature began to appear. The most articulate rejoinder (and one that other newspapers trumpeted), came from the *Fort Worth Gazette* and was titled "The Higher Law." Below is a short excerpt:

> The theory of the governor's message to the legislature, based on the Paris holocaust, is correct, but it is most unhappily timed and does injustice to the people of Paris and to the citizenship aggregate of the state. The impression that will be given abroad

by the message is not warranted by the situation anywhere in the state. The governor is charged with the enforcement of the laws, and he is also morally responsible for the reputation of the state to the extent that it is affected by his official acts. Before lending the prestige of his office in support of the bitterest charges made against Texas people by their most malignant enemies, he should have considered the subject in a more moderate spirit than is displayed in his message... There is no animal which is not susceptible to the sensation of fear. It is not likely that any being in Lamar County, with the stature and appearance of a man will tempt the fate of Henry Smith.

Others remote from that locality who have the propensities of Smith should be taught to keep his fate in mind rather than that his executioners were as guilty as himself. Let them beware. The next brute in Texas to commit Smith's crime, whether he be white or black, rich or poor, will, if captured, be ushered through the gates of the damned in some such unpleasant manner as that which sent Smith there. Neither governor's proclamations nor jeremiads from the press can prevent it. The people of Texas know how to protect their homes, and by all that is held sacred there, they are going to do it if it offends against every letter in every sentence of every act of all the legislatures of Christendom.

On February 9, the *Gazette*—a publication for which the Henry Smith lynching had arguably become a cause *celebre*—commented again, publishing a large, vertical, two-scene editorial cartoon addressing the ongoing controversy. In the top section, the Goddess of Liberty (who at that time had only been sitting atop the Capitol Dome in Austin for five years) was standing with one foot on a book of "Law" and one on the sword of "Justice," pointing toward Henry Smith smoldering on the stake while holding a torch to guide her through the "Dark Ages" the lynching had presumably placed Texas in. The caption under the depiction asked "Has Civilization Gone Mad?" In the lower panel, an African American man (Smith) was holding a bloody knife in one hand and standing with one foot on the corpse of a young babe (Myrtle Vance). The caption under it read "Civilization Has Gone Mad." The cartoon suggested that if Texans lived in a world where black men could kill young white girls, society was lost and the folks of Paris simply employed a corrective measure.

Debate over the Smith lynching would continue for weeks and

The Paris Horror

A vertical-paneled editorial cartoon that countered the notion that the Smith lynching was evidence of "Civilization Gone Mad." *Fort Worth Gazette*, 1893.

immediately begin informing other lynchings. On July 7, 1893, an African American named Charles Miller was reported to be burned at the stake in Bardwell, Kentucky. According to the July 8 edition of the *Evening Democrat*:

> Charles Miller, the alleged murderer of the two Bay sisters was burned alive here yesterday afternoon before an immense crowd of people from all parts of the country within 200 miles. A large pile of wood with the wretched, breathless fiend incarnate on the top was built and the Paris, Tex., affair was duplicated.

The citizens of Bardwell had wanted to duplicate the "Paris" affair, but the *Evening Democrat* got the outcome wrong. They actually lynched Miller with a noose because there was some doubt as to his guilt. In the end, that doubt was warranted; Miller was later found to have been innocent.

One month later, when an African American man named Henry Runnels allegedly murdered members of a white family (R. H. Marsh, his wife—whom was also raped—and their ten-year-old son) a duplication of the Smith lynching was considered in Montgomery, Texas. As reported in the *Dallas Morning News*, "The Paris roasting was talked of in sepulchral whispers and it was declared that he [Runnels] deserved a worse fate even than did Smith, the murderer of little Myrtle Vance." The citizens of Montgomery were split on whether to apply the noose or the torch and one white woman was cheered for volunteering to burn the suspect herself; but the noose faction prevailed and Runnels was hanged.

In late 1893, an exculpatory, 200-page book titled *The Facts in the Case of the Horrible Murder of Little Myrtle Vance and its Fearful Expiation at Paris, Texas, February 1, 1893* was published by P. L. James (in Paris, Texas) "for the Benefit of the Family of Henry Vance" and copyrighted by Henry Vance. It was a flimsy, homespun attempt to exonerate Vance and the entire city of Paris, but it didn't hold up in terms of credibility or longevity. That being said, it was far more legitimate than *An Eye for An Eye or The Fiend and the Fagot: An Unvarnished Account of the Burning of Henry Smith at Paris, Texas, February 1, 1893, and the Reason he was Tortured*, also published in 1893 by Junius M. Early. *An Eye for An Eye* claimed that Henry Smith's crime "will so freeze you that only the flames in which the criminal was burned could ever warm your blood to run again." Early was a local real estate salesman and the seventy-page account was little more than a heavily varnished pamphlet with ads in the front and back and a concluding poetic canto.

Governor Hogg continued in his campaign to compel the Texas legislature to enact anti-lynching laws in response to Smith's horrendous execution, but his efforts and entreaties were largely ignored. At a speech in Rockdale, Texas, on October 1, 1894, Hogg was blunt:

> The wanton, cruel, unhuman execution of defenseless citizens and prisoners by murderous bands of criminals is an outrage upon civilization that should be summarily suppressed. . . Lynchers are murderers, Mobs are bands of murderers. Murderers should have their necks broken. This is the way to stop them.

On December 12, 1898, Henry Vance "dropped dead" in a Paris saloon. According to newspaper reports, Vance had been "mentally afflicted" ever since the Smith lynching and "periodically resorted to extreme intoxication," a proclivity that hastened his demise.

In early June of 1901, a Pittsburgh, Kansas curio specialist named O. P. Bailey reportedly added a coveted artifact to his collection: "a piece of fence rail about eighteen inches long which it is claimed was taken from the fire that burned the negro in Paris, Texas." According to reports, "blood stains can yet be seen upon the side that is not charred by fire."

The lynching of Henry Smith remained a morbid spectacle in the minds and imaginations of many Americans for decades to come. But as late as 1930, *Palestine Daily Herald* editor Alexander Neville was still defending the efficacy of the Smith execution, insisting that it had been a profound deterrent because no other (presumably white) children had been abducted, brutalized or murdered in the vicinity of Paris since.

II.

1861

White Texans specialized in burning blacks alive.
> Walter L. Buenger
> *Southwestern Historical Quarterly*
> Volume 103, July 1999 - April 2000

Henry Smith was not the first or last person of color to be burned at the stake in Texas—his incineration was simply the most notorious and influential. An accurate list of how many persons of color (mostly African American) white Texans dispatched with fire is probably impossible, but an examination of newspaper records, memoirs, letters and interviews provide a rudimentary picture.

It can be established that Texans burned more people of color at the stake than almost any other state in America and as many as most of the other states combined. It can be established that folks in the state of Texas burned at least thirty-two people of color (thirty-one African Americans and one Mexican) at the stake between 1891 and 1922 (and at least nine besides, in the years before and after that period), averaging over one a year for thirty years. And it can be established from the existing historical record that Texas staged two of the most largely spectated burnings at the stake in American history, one being that of Henry Smith and another being that of Jessie Washington.

The first recorded African American burned at the stake in Texas was named "Green." Records are scant, but he was apparently a slave belonging to J. V. Rogers near Marshall.

On September 8, 1861, a twelve-year-old white girl named Martha McLellan was reportedly pulled from her horse while returning from a neighbor's house. The young girl, described as "intelligent" and "interesting," was allegedly dragged from her mount, raped and then brutally murdered.

When the evening came and Martha still hadn't made it home, her father, James, organized a search party and discovered her body near a roadside. Her throat had also apparently been slit.

James McLellan hired Green on loan (from Rogers) to assist in the search, which Green did, but reportedly nonchalantly; and that made him suspicious. From there the determination of his guilt can be no better related than it was presented in the *Marshall Texas Republican*:

> But a righteous heaven never intended that such a crime should remain undiscovered or unpunished. Circumstances led to the belief that he [Green] had committed the deed, and upon being arraigned and charged with it, he confessed his guilt. The neighbors determined, upon consultation, that he merited the most severe punishment that could be inflicted, and on Monday evening they burned him at the stake.

Other than Green's search party dispassion, the "circumstances" that led to his backwoods indictment are not made clear. His guilt appeared to be as much divined as established, until his confession, which—like many African American confessions then and up until very recently—was probably coerced.

Forced confessions would practically become a rule for white lynch mobs. Though they had no qualms about suspending due process or denying proper legal representation to their victims, they remained sticklers about offering a primitive semblance of justice or at least vengeance. If nothing else was above reproach, they could at least raise high a confession, reliable or no.

Green was burned at the stake and lost to history.

1863

The negro had murdered his master. All the negroes on the plantations were rounded up, and compelled to witness the burning. The guilty man begged for mercy, but a relentless mob chained him to a stake, put pine wood about his black body, poured oil on his quivering head and set him afire. It was a terrifying sight. Soldiers on horseback corralled shrieking negro spectators; the negro screamed as the flames licked his body. I was only about eight years old—but it was the most gruesome sight I have ever seen.

> Daniel Washington Harris Buzbee
> *Abilene Reporter-News*
> **January 22, 1945**

In April of 1863, a male slave named "Rube" was burned at the stake southeast of Paris, Texas.

Rube belonged to former Lamar County tax collector, Mitchell Henderson McCuistion. As the story goes, a female slave asked Rube to kill her mistress, Margaret McCuistion (Mitchell's wife), because she was going to have her whipped. Mrs. McQuistion was subsequently killed while attempting to take a letter from her husband (who was off fighting for the Confederacy) to his aged mother. She was found with her throat cut on the bank of a nearby creek and Rube was forthwith suspicioned. The rest is detailed in *Palestine Daily Herald* editor Alexander Neville's book, *The Red River Valley Then and Now* (1948):

> There was no thought of appealing to the court, for the crime was one calling for swift punishment. At least 75 men, all old because the young men were in the Army, and a number of women and children were in the crowd. It was determined that the Negro must die and the method was put to a vote of all present. The vote was 46 for burning at the stake and 36 advocated hanging,

1863

so he was fastened to a post, wood piled about him, and burned until nothing was left but ashes and some charred bones.

It could not be called mob action, for it was open and done in daylight.

The female slave Rube allegedly killed Mrs. McCuistion to protect was reportedly "given a terrible whipping" anyway.[12]

1867

This outrage cries to Heaven, to God and man for vengeance. The laws must be vindicated. Life and property must be protected, the lawless spirit now running wild through the State must be put down, the lives of freedmen must be secured and protected, if our own people fail to do it, we will rejoice to see it done by Federal authority.

Crockett Sentinel
February 19, 1867

On February 16, 1867, two unidentified African American men were burned to death in Leon County, Texas.

After the Civil War, many of the African Americans who had worked on G. K. Cessna's plantation (three miles west of Alabama Landing) remained and continued their labor as freedmen. On February 16—while Cessna himself was absent—a small contingent of white men laid siege to the freedmen living at the Cessna place, gunning two down in cold blood and killing two others by burning the cabin they inhabited to the ground. One made it out of the fire but died after being "completely roasted." The other perished inside the structure, the blaze reducing him to charred bones.

Some of the surviving freedmen were able to identify the white men behind the incident, but the perpetrators fled to escape prosecution at the hands of a Reconstruction judiciary.

Reconstruction officials were undeterred and their effort was quickly supplemented. According to the *Centreville Conservative*, the Union Commander of Texas himself, General Charles Griffin,[13] ordered Capt. Reinhard to confiscate enough of the perpetrators' property "to indemnify the losses sustained by negroes in the outrage committed upon Mr. Cessna's plantation."

The order required that two hundred dollars should be paid to the families of each of the adults who were killed, and that the Capts. Reinhard and Bradford should assess the amount of damages sustained by each of the negroes upon the plantation, all of which, together with the amount assessed by Gen. Griffin for the indemnification of the families in the loss of their heads, was to be paid by confiscation and sale of property.

General Griffin fell victim to a yellow fever epidemic in southeast Texas seven months later and died on September 15, 1867.

As soon as the Reconstruction period ended, white Texans rolled back most of the gains that freedmen had made in the region and re-instituted a system of civic impropriety based on white primacy.

1876

Judge Lynch makes mistakes, of course, but his charges are moderate and his aim is always to inflict swift punishment upon the guilty.

San Marcos Free Press
July 26, 1883

On January 20, 1876, an African American man named Anthony Smith was burned at the stake just north of Cameron in Milam County.

Nine days earlier, twenty-three-year-old Smith had reportedly been observed riding on a bay pony not too far behind a Bell County cotton farmer named John M. Baker. Baker had traveled to Rockdale by wagon to sale a bale of cotton and a few hides. When he turned up dead, a witness testified that he saw a black man shoot Baker in the back and then circle around and shoot him from the front. The assailant then allegedly robbed Baker's corpse.

On January 13, Smith—who was reportedly still in possession of Baker's money and one of his personal effects—was captured and brought to Rockdale by Milam County Deputy Sheriff Pete Turner. Smith was subsequently transferred to the Milam County seat in Cameron and indicted for murder in the first degree. Smith's trial was presided over by well-regarded District Judge Andrew Sidney Broaddus[14] and the appointed jury found him guilty in less than a week, sentencing him to hang thirty days hence.

On January 20, however, before dawn, a group of forty to fifty vigilantes (most thought to be the victim's friends and relatives from Bell County) rode on the Milam County jail. Sheriff William E. Mitchusson had gone home the evening before and left the jail in the charge of a deputy named William Sherod Robinson. Robinson (who would later be lynched himself after trying to rob a bank in

Medicine Lodge, Kansas) immediately relinquished his gun and the jail keys and let the lynching party take Smith.

The vigilantes transported Smith a few miles north of Cameron to a mesquite thicket. There they tied his hands and secured them above his head to the trees and, according to some reports, fired at his feet, making him dance. Then they gathered kindling and a load of wood and set a fire beneath him.

The lynching party watched the fire build to a blaze and cook Smith to a crisp. Then they riddled his burnt remains with bullets.

Though Texas Governor Richard Coke involved Assistant Attorney General A. J. Peeler in a brief (if not perfunctory) investigation of the incident, the members of the lynching party were never identified. Judge Broaddus told the *Galveston Daily News* that the act comprised an "unparalleled case of lawlessness," especially as the state's laws and the court system had performed properly and without delay. Critics of the legal process in the case were reportedly happy with the verdict and the sentencing, but not the thirty-day wait for an execution.

Sheriff Mitchusson resigned on February 15, 1876. His family later claimed that he had never been comfortable with the evidence against Smith and was unhappy with the verdict and outraged by the lynching.

1890

> History is heavily edited for school-children and, for most of us, commencement puts an end to study. Thus we go through life with notions of our past which, for depth, complexity, subtlety of shading, rank with comic books. Texas history particularly lends itself to this; it is so farfetched that only a child would believe it.
>
> **William Humphrey**
> *No Resting Place* **(1990)**

On December 14, 1890, an African American man named John Joiner was burned to death in the Kerens jail.

According to reports in the *Fort Worth Gazette* and the *McKinney Democrat*, Joiner spent the evening of December 13 "drinking heavily" and, just before nightfall, ill-advisedly climbed onto another man's horse, attempting to leave town. Joiner was quickly "intercepted" by the Kerens marshal and placed in the town "calaboose" (jail) for horse theft or public drunkenness. Then:

> Some time afterward parties on the street noticed the calaboose to be on fire, but as it is seldom used were in no haste to give the alarm. When they finally reached the burning building they supposed that no one was in it, but after it was consumed they found the charred trunks of the negro among the debris, burned beyond recognition. It is supposed in his drunken, maudlin state he set fire to the building himself.

Besides the fact that this account presupposes that Joiner had something to start a fire with, it arguably also relies on a conspicuous level of credulity. If Joiner was sober enough to attempt to burn his way out of a jailhouse, wouldn't he also have been sober enough to scream as passersby witnessed the disastrous outcome?

At best, Joiner's death was the result of gross negligence (as jailhouses usually employed jailors who monitored the facilities and

1890

their inhabitants)—but the possibility that Joiner's horrific death was not an accident obviously warrants consideration.

1891

The Constitution recognizes the equality of the negroes; but for them that Constitution is the greatest of political fictions. The letter of the law excludes them from no position; but race is stronger than law, and the spirit in which the law is administered is such that there is no common ground for them and the whites.

London Times
January 21, 1891

On October 26, 1891, an African American known as Lee Green[15] was burned at the stake in Cass County, Texas.

Green, an eighteen-year-old mulatto, was employed by a white man named John Lowe near Douglassville. On October 24, while John was at the local cotton gin, Green allegedly murdered Mrs. Lowe and threw her body in the Lowe well. He followed the mother's body with her infant babe and then chased the Lowe's five-year-old son around the property until he jumped in the well to escape. Green then reportedly threw a wash tub into the well (to be thorough) and then returned to the Lowe house to plunder a trunk where he knew Mr. Lowe kept his money.

Green supposedly took $60 and made his escape on a mule.

When John returned home his family was missing and his house was bloodstained and ransacked. He eventually rescued his son from the well and heard the chilling details regarding his wife's and their baby's deaths. As word spread, search parties were formed and began combing the area.

Green took refuge at the home of an unwitting African American family he was familiar with, but when the patriarch of the family caught wind of Green's possible involvement in the murders, he had no choice but to turn him in. He contacted Cass County Deputy Sheriff Clement Galaway and had him remove Green from his

1891

home. Galaway transported Green to the county jail in Linden. The sheriff, Isaac H. Lanier, was still out searching for Green, unaware of his capture.

When members of other search parties heard tell of Green's incarceration in Linden, they proceeded straight to the jail, and, in the sheriff's absence, were confronted by his wife. They restrained her, took the jail keys and then seized Green and transported him to the scene of the crime in Douglassville. Several African Americans that had been involved in the pursuit fell in with the procession. When the growing lynch-mob and Green reached Douglassville, the murderer reportedly confessed.

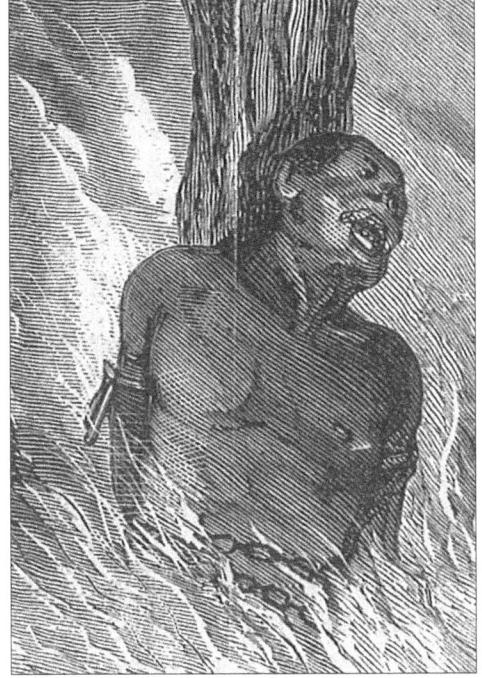

A depiction of an African American man burned at the stake. *Frank Leslie's Illustrated Newspaper*, 1868.

After his confession, an old white woman secured Green to a persimmon tree with a trace chain.[16] Then forty-six African American men placed wood and kindling in a pile around Green until it reached his neck.

Over a thousand people (white and black) had congregated to see the lynching, and the match that ignited the fire (delivering what the *Galveston Daily News* later called "An Awful Expiation") was applied by an "old colored woman."[17]

When Texas Governor James S. Hogg (who had only been in office for nine months—the lynching of Henry Smith would occur just over a year later) learned of the lynching, he issued a proclamation and offered rewards. It was published in the November 4, 1891 edition of Linden's *Alliance Standard* newspaper:

> WHEREAS, it has been made known to me that on the 26th day of October, A. D. 1891, in the county of Cass, unknown persons constituting a mob did take one Lee Green (a negro) from the

jail of said county and did murder him; and that said unknown persons are now at large and fugitives from justice.

    Now, therefore, I, J. S. Hogg, Governor of the State of Texas, do, by virtue of the authority vested in me by the constitution and laws of this State, hereby offer a reward of ONE THOUSAND DOLLARS for the arrest and conviction of the leaders of said mob and TWO HUNDRED DOLLARS for the arrest of other principals, accomplices and accessories and the delivery of said leaders, and principals, accomplices and accessories to the Sheriff of Cass County, Texas, inside the jail door of said county, within six months from this day, and conviction thereafter.

And in a letter informing Sheriff Lanier of his offer (also published in the *Standard*), Governor Hogg minced no words in his criticism of the incident:

> There is no room for mobs in Texas, and they must cease their crime raids if any virtue clings to established government. They are a menace to the life and liberty of every unprotected citizen; they are enemies to the Bill of Rights; they are incubators and propagators of crime, visiting vengeance on the defenseless, often the innocent, striking down the bulwarks of liberty and laying waste to civilization.

There is no evidence that any folks in the region took Governor Hogg up on his offer.

The names of the white and black matriarchs singularly involved in the burning of Lee Green are now lost to history, but their roles and the ethnic make-up of the lynching party were peculiar unless, perhaps, one considers what happened in Comanche County just five years prior.

    In late July, 1886, in the town of Comanche, an African American man named Tom McNeel allegedly murdered a pregnant, white woman named Sallie Stephens. A white mob lynched McNeel and then banished every black inhabitant of Comanche County. The crime Green committed in Douglassville may simply have been as appalling and offensive to the local black citizenry as it was to the white citizenry; but if the black citizenry hadn't take part in the lynching, it's entirely plausible that they might have suffered the same fate as the black inhabitants of Comanche County.

1892

The epidemic of African lust that has lately taken such hideous feature must give pause to the hopes of thoughtful negroes who have set their hearts upon the speedy and universal exaltation of the race. The atavism of ancient bestiality—which in greater or less degree was a quality of all races in their primitive stages—seems to have suddenly redeveloped in a few Herculean sons of Ham a fiendish carnality for Caucasian beauty.

Galveston Daily News
August 8, 1893

On February 20, 1892, an African American man named Ed Coy was burned at the stake in Texarkana, Arkansas. He is included in this list because his executioners had originally intended to lynch him at the Texas-Arkansas state line in Texarkana and there is little doubt that some of the participants in this lynching were Texas citizens.

Coy was accused of raping the wife of a white farmer named Henry W. Jewell on February 13, 1892. When made aware of the charges, Coy fled and hid at the home of another African American man named Ed Gaines. On Saturday, February 20, Coy was captured and presented to Mrs. (Julia) Jewell for identification. Mrs. Jewell identified him as her assailant and he was guarded until all the search parties who had been combing the countryside for him returned.

Coy was then marched to a telegraph pole at the most public place in the city. It sat on Broad Street at the Texas-Arkansas state boundary.

The lynch-mob's original intent was to hang Coy from the telegraph pole, but a large percentage of the mob felt that a hanging wasn't enough and that he should suffer the torch "to strike terror to the hearts of the negroes." The noose proponents acquiesced, but on the condition that Coy be burned outside the city limits. The mob marched Coy in a southeasterly direction and found an open field with an upright, ten-foot tall tree-stump in it (probably less than a mile from the Texas-Arkansas state line). Members of the mob affixed Coy to the stump and then doused him in coal oil. Then they summoned Mrs. Jewell to face her alleged ravager and strike the match that would punish the crime.

Mrs. Jewell was assisted by male relatives to the tree stump to which Coy was bound. She approached her alleged attacker in a psychological fog and lit him on fire emotionlessly. The white crowd gasped with delight, but Coy apparently exhibited "wonderful nerve" as the flames consumed him.[18] A *Dallas Morning News* correspondent spoke with Coy before his lynching and reported that the suspect maintained that he was innocent "and died with the lie on his lips."

The incident was later investigated by Albion W. Tourgee,[19] a white, former circuit court judge and future litigant for the plaintiff in *Plessy v. Ferguson*. Tourgee came to the following conclusions:

1. The woman who was paraded as a victim of violence was of bad character; her husband was a drunk and gambler.
2. She was publicly reported and generally known to have been criminally intimate with Coy for more than a year previous.
3. She was compelled by threats, if not violence, to make the charge against the victim.
4. When she came to apply the match Coy asked her if she would burn him after they had "been sweethearting" so long.
5. A large majority of the "superior" white men prominent in the affair are the reputed fathers of mulatto children.

    These are not pleasant facts, but they are illustrative of the vital phase of the so-called race question, which should properly be designated an earnest inquiry as to the best methods by which religion, science, law and political power may be employed to excuse injustice, barbarity and crime done to a people because of race and color.

Today the story of Ed Coy and Julia Jewell is part of a Texarkana "Ghost Walks" tour that takes place every Saturday night, weather permitting. Guides suggest Coy's ghost still haunts the community seeking justice.

1895

A couple of fakirs were in town Monday and Tuesday with an outfit representing the execution of Henry Smith, at Paris, by the mob. Such events as the burning of Smith should be forgotten as speedily as possible, and anything calculated to keep it alive in the public mind should be discountenanced.

Shiner Gazette
December 12, 1893

On October 29, 1895—in the first reported Texas burning at the stake since Henry Smith's torture and lynching in Paris—an African American man was burned at the stake in Tyler, Texas. The *Fort Worth Daily Gazette*, the *Gainesville Daily Hesperian* and the *San Antonio El Regidor* identified him as Henry Hillard; the *Dallas Morning News*, the *Galveston Daily News*, the *McKinney Democrat*, the *Marshall Evening Messenger* and the *Wills Point Chronicle* referred to him as Jim King. This account will defer to the minority, because an important later chronicle refers to him as Robert Hillard.

Reports are insufficient, but from the accounts that are available, Henry (or Robert) Hillard was the only suspect in the rape and murder of Mrs. Leonard Bell, the nineteen-year-old wife of successful local farmer. How the suspicion of Hillard as Mrs. Bell's murderer was ever established is unclear, especially as she—the only eyewitness besides her attacker—was dead. But the newspaper narratives apparently ignored this issue and picked right up with Hillard's guilt.

After Hillard's guilt was introduced, the *Daily Hesperian* (of Gainesville) offered an account of his alleged confession:

> I was coming down the road and saw Mrs. Bell in the road. She was afraid of me, and I knew that if I passed her she would say I tried to rape her, and I concluded that I would rape her and then

Stereographic image of Henry Hillard (hatless) "In the Hands of the Mob."
Courtesy of Library of Congress.

kill her. I cut her throat and then cut her in another place and left.

After Hillard allegedly raped and murdered Mrs. Bell, he reportedly fled east. On October 29 at around 4 a.m., he was discovered asleep in a cotton pen three miles shy of Kilgore and surrendered without incident.

The arresting committee, led by Smith County Sheriff Wig Smith, was trailed by several dozen armed vigilantes and when authorities transported the suspect to the crime scene, they were met by hundreds (some accounts say 2,000) of additional vigilantes. Between the two vengeful assemblages, the authorities were forced to give up their prisoner.

Once in control, the mob reportedly verified Hillard's identity and decided to vote on what his punishment should be and where it should take place. A burning at the stake in the city of Tyler's public square carried the day.

With Hillard in tow, the mob proceeded to the agreed upon ex-

Stereographic image of Henry Hillard affixed to the stake after the "First Fire Withdrawn." The mob semi-extinguished and rekindled the fire at intervals to make Hillard's suffering worse. *Courtesy of Library of Congress.*

ecution location and arrived at 4 p.m.; a crowd of thousands was waiting. By 4:30 p.m. a makeshift scaffold was constructed on the west side of the public square and wagons were brought in with ample amounts of wood, straw and coal oil.

Hillard was escorted to the scaffold and afforded an opportunity to speak, but the crowd was so loud his comments were inaudible. He was permitted a moment to pray and then affixed to an iron rail that ran vertically through the makeshift scaffold. Mr. Bell subsequently appeared and applied the match to the kindling under the scaffold. Within moments, Hillard was enveloped in "sheets of fire."

Hillard begged for mercy, but his entreaties fell on deaf ears. Onlookers threw "burning missiles" at him, but instead of allowing the conflagration to consume him and end his misery, his executioners were careful to partially extinguish it at short intervals and then re-fire it again to ensure maximum agony. Each time the flames subsided, Hillard believed his torment was done, but a torch-bearer revived the blaze. Hillard eventually began trying to end his own life, first by attempting to swallow the flames when they grew high and, failing that, trying to bash his head in by slamming it backwards on the iron rail.

Sheriff Smith had wired the governor before the lynching, but neither man was able to stop it. The makeshift scaffold became Hillard's funeral pyre and his physical form was reduced to brittle cinder.

The Barnum & Baily's circus arrived in Tyler the next day, and every participant was ushered to the dark spot on the west side of the public plaza. The circus troupe was later hard-pressed to perform anything as compelling as the slow roast of Henry Hillard the night before.

When African Americans were questioned regarding the manner of Hillard's execution, they reportedly endorsed it, but there was presumably no other way they could safely respond. The prevailing white sentiment regarding Hillard's fate was conveyed in the November 1 edition of the *Fort Worth Daily Gazette*:

> The work of burning the negro was not done by any mob of infuriated men, but by the best citizens of East Texas, coolly and deliberately. The governor of the state, in the performance of his duty, was [is] compelled to follow the mandate of the law and have an investigation made and an attempt made to apply the

law. These people will fail. Smith county officers did all in their power, but they were toys in the hands of 10,000 people.

Some newspapers identified Henry Hillard as Jim King. Appearing under a headline of "Roasted to Death," this illustration depicted the burning of King (Hillard) at the stake. *Dallas Morning News,* 1895.

The *Daily Hesperian* echoed the *Daily Gazette's* sentiments and placed Mrs. Bell's murder in a familiar context: "The crime this negro committed is the most horrible in the history of this section, and equal in horror to the murder of the little Vance girl at Paris."

In 1897, two entrepreneurs (identified in a February 4, 1897 copyright deposit as Breckenridge & Scruggs) created a sixteen-image set of stereographic cards that portray the murder of Mrs. Bell, Hillard's capture by bloodhounds and his subsequent burning at the stake on a downtown street in Tyler. The early stills are staged and feature hand-colored blood and actors; the later ones include actual images of Hillard. The photographs were taken by C. A. Davis and the set is stored at the Library of Congress in Washington, D. C.

1901

It is a fact that in the period between the burning of the Negro at Paris, Texas, and the present time there have been more of these horrors committed than at any period of the same length before. It is also a fact that never before has the punishment been so sure, speedy and dreadful... Death, even by fire, has no terrors for these wretches, because their intelligence is so low that they are incapable of imagining the pangs of cremation.

> L. B. de Pontes
> *Houston Post*
> **September 6, 1901**

On Wednesday, March 13, 1901, a twenty-two-year-old African American man named Jonas "John" Henderson was burned at the stake in Corsicana, Texas.

Seven days earlier, a white woman named Valley Dale Younger was brutally murdered at her home and her death was apparently witnessed by her two children. According to the *Dallas Times Herald*, her kids claimed "A big negro knocked mama down and dragged her away." Valley's body was found by her father approximately 150 feet from her home and her husband Conway formed a search party with some neighbors and procured bloodhounds.

For the next few days, the search party—which came to include Navarro County law enforcement personnel—zigzagged back and forth in a westward direction. On Monday, March 11, they took Henderson (who was a big "Negro") into custody near Hillsboro.

Back in Corsicana, plans for a lynching were already in the works and Henderson's legally appointed captors were weary of returning. They contacted McLennan County Sheriff J. W. Baker in Waco and asked if Henderson could be transferred there until a trial could be arranged, but Baker said no. Henderson spent the night in the Hillsboro jail and the next day Governor Joseph D. Sayers got

1901

John Henderson being led from the Navarro County Jail by a chain around his neck. Note the white scratches over the faces of most of the escort; as if someone attempted to conceal their identities. *From the collections of the Texas/Dallas History Archives Division of the Dallas Public Library.*

word to law enforcement officials instructing them to transport him to Fort Worth.

On Tuesday, March 12, Navarro County Constable W. B. Grantham, a Navarro County Deputy Sheriff named Hammond and Bell County Sheriff Sam Sparks boarded a northbound train in Hillsboro with Henderson and headed to Fort Worth. Just before the train arrived at the Itasca stop, several armed Corsicana citizens (who had also boarded the train in Hillsboro) got the drop on Henderson's escort and seized him. The vigilantes transported Henderson forty-five miles back to Corsicana by horseback and placed him in the Navarro County jail in the custody of newly elected sheriff Wiley B. Robinson.

The next morning, a committee including Precinct 1 Justice of the Peace H. G. Roberts visited Henderson and "determined" his guilt, at which point Henderson reportedly inscribed his "X" (he could neither read nor write) to a signed confession and dictated a letter to his father.

Corsicana leaders making speeches before the lynching of John Henderson.
From the collections of the Texas/Dallas History Archives Division of the Dallas Public Library.

Informalities complete, the committee decided Henderson should be burned at the stake at 2 p.m. When news arrived that Texas Rangers and state militia were en route from Dallas, the committee moved the execution time up to 11 a.m.

The lynch-mob's staging group drove a trolley car rail into the ground on one side of the Navarro County courthouse, stacked boxes and lumber around it and then saturated the kindling with coal oil. Near the assigned hour, Sheriff Robinson was warned to remain at the jail and several men escorted Henderson by chain from the jailhouse to the steel rail in the yard. As Henderson was fastened to the stake with wire and chains, the Corsicana fire bell rang to summon folks from the surrounding stores and businesses. Just before the fire was lit, Conway Younger approached Henderson and slashed him across the face with a knife.

After Henderson was aflame, Conway attempted to slash him again and several women from the Younger neighborhood reportedly threw wood into the fire as it blazed, conspicuously aiming for Henderson's head.

1901

Emitting nary a whimper, Henderson was dead within ten minutes. The mob dispersed quietly and memento seekers sifted through the charred remains.

Judge Roberts subsequently performed an "inquest," but it resembled more a coronation of the affair rather than a coroner's report:

> I find that the deceased came to his just death at the hands of the incensed and outraged feelings of the best people in the United States, the citizens of Navarro and adjoining counties. The evidence, as well as the confession of guilt by deceased, shows that his punishment was fully merited and commendable.

A crowded, northbound train arrived in Corsicana at noon and its passengers were disappointed to find they that had missed the spectacle. The rumored Texas Ranger and state militia forces never materialized. Governor Sayers' Adjutant General, Thomas Scurry, had dispatched a telegraph to Corsicana-area state militia Colonel G. W. Hardy before the lynching ordering him to muster the local militia to prevent it; but Hardy protested that the 500 men he could

Corsicana mob erecting the stake that John Henderson was burned at. *From the collections of the Texas/Dallas History Archives Division of the Dallas Public Library.*

Corsicana mob watches as John Henderson's remains burn at the stake. *From the collections of the Texas/Dallas History Archives Division of the Dallas Public Library.*

muster would be no match for the mob and comprise an impetus for further bloodshed. Hardy petitioned Scurry to summon the militias in Mexia, Waco and Dallas to assist, but the incident concluded before the suggested coordination could be implemented.

Incongruities in Henderson's alleged confession and letter to his father later raised questions and today it is generally suspected that Henderson may not have realized what he was confessing to when he inscribed his "X."

A book titled, *Navarro County History* published "Under The Auspices Of The Navarro County Historical Society" in 1975 devotes a small chapter to the last official hanging in the county in 1902, but makes no reference to the more notorious and arguably more significant lynching of John Henderson in 1901. Sheriff Wiley Robinson was present at the hanging and served as the official executioner.

Five months after Henderson met his end in Corsicana, an African American man named Abe Wildner was burned at the stake near

1901

Red Branch (Grayson County) on August 20, 1901.

Wildner was accused of assaulting and murdering the nineteen-year-old, newlywed wife of J. M. Caldwell, a farmer who lived near Whitesboro. Reports varied, but the general storyline suggested that Wildner had visited the Caldwell residence on August 16 and then later returned the same day, observing from afar until he saw Mr. Caldwell depart.

After Mr. Caldwell was gone, Wildner presumably called on Mrs. Caldwell with an "indecent proposal." It was pure speculation, but investigators assumed Mrs. Caldwell ordered Wildner to leave, he attacked her and she fought back. According to one account, Wildner knocked her unconscious with an ax handle, sexually assaulted her and then slit her throat. When Mr. Caldwell returned around 6 p.m., he found his new bride's dead body in their cellar. As Wildner had reportedly visited the Caldwell residence earlier in the day, he was the only suspect.

Mr. Caldwell and his neighbors began searching for Wildner in every direction, but he was nowhere to be found. The *Southern Mercury* newspaper (out of Dallas) would later issue a description:

> He is about 5 feet 9 or 10 inches high, weighs 150 or 160 pounds, is slightly lame in one leg and limps noticeably, has the appearance of a laborer and has worked in coal mines, is of a gingerbread color. When last seen he had on a small, raw-edged, narrow-brim black hat, buckskin band, was in his shirtsleeves, had on a pair of black pants, and also had a pair of blue overalls, which he may wear over the pants. He had a pair of No. 6 shoes, which, being to small, are likely to be cut at the sides.[20]

Like Henry Smith, Abe Wildner apparently eluded searchers for days. On August 20, he was captured near Mud Creek in the Chickasaw Nation (southern Oklahoma) by three farmers. By the time the farmers got Wildner close to the state line, their numbers had increased tenfold and the size of the transport swelled even more as they continued south. The search efforts they encountered along the way folded into their ranks.

Meanwhile, as word of Wildner's capture spread through Grayson County, two parties expressed considerable interest. The first was Governor Joseph D. Sayers.

Governor Sayers mustered state militias in Gainesville and Denison, instructing them to find, secure and protect Wildner so as to afford him due process. The second keenly interested party was the large percentage of the white population in Grayson County that was diametrically opposed to Wildner's right of due process. While Governor Sayers was mobilizing militias to prevent a lynching in Whitesboro, folks from all over Grayson and the surrounding counties began pouring into the town to see a lynching (which was probably being billed as a sequel to the Paris "holocaust").

Right before Wildner's mob-escort re-entered Texas near Dexter in Cooke County, they received news of the called up militias and held up at the Red River. There, they appear to have been accosted by Grayson County authorities, but not in sufficient enough numbers to take control of the procession. The vigilante escort decided to avoid Dexter and proceed to Grayson County as swiftly as possible.

Once in Grayson County, the vigilante-escort (which, again, included law enforcement personnel under some level of protest) decided that proceeding to Whitesboro would endanger their opportunity for summary justice, so they headed towards Red Branch. There they reportedly stopped at a large elm tree on William Columbus Nelson's ranch, but what happened next is unclear.

The accounts of Grayson County law enforcement officials differ from those of some of the vigilantes. Some reports say Wildner confessed; others say he didn't. Some testimonies say Wildner claimed he was "crazed with drink" when he killed Mrs. Caldwell; others indicate he gave no details and was stoic throughout his entire lynching.

Some narratives indicate Wildner was hanged until dead while a fire was burning under him. Other accounts say Wildner was repeatedly hanged and burned and raised and lowered to prolong his sufferings. The *El Paso Herald* report, entitled "Human Torch: Fearful Torture Suffered by a Negro Brute for 'the Usual Crime,'" paints a horrific picture:

> But this death was too merciful in the opinion of some of the mob and the fire was allowed to die down, the negro's blackened body was lowered, and the rope removed from his neck. The writhing of the half-burned animal was jeered by the mob, who seemed to enjoy the brief respite, it was so much more horrible than mere cremation.

The *Herald* and the *Dallas Morning News* reported that the lynching party paused so long at one point that members were able to ride to a nearby community and get more coal oil. In the meantime, while Wildner presumably smoldered in a semi-state of consciousness, the lynch-mob piled up more wood.

When the additional coal oil arrived, the vigilantes soaked Wildner and the new woodpile in it and re-hanged him. Then, according to the *Herald*, the vigilantes re-lit the fire and watched:

> The oil blazed up, and almost enveloped the scene in the lurid flame. The odor of roasting human flesh was sickening, and the writhing body in dying convulsions made the sparks fly.

The blaze subsequently reduced what was left of Wildner to cinder and ash.

Back in Whitesboro crowds reacted with disappointment to news of what they considered a premature vengeance. Thousands remained out in the public square awaiting further news; others headed home grumbling.

The epilogue of the unprosecuted crime and lynching was a new Whitesboro decree. As reported in the *Dallas Morning News*, "All negroes who do not own property or have a good, established character, have been warned to leave Whitesboro, and the last one of the objectionable characters left today, and all those who live here were ordered not to allow any strange negroes to come in here, as they will be badly treated."

In 1903 the remaining African American community in Whitesboro was reportedly driven out after two white women alleged that they were nearly attacked by two African American men.

1902

Why is it that a civilized community will permit negroes to be burned at the stake? Are we retrograding to a primitive condition of life, that the passions must be satisfied by deeds that were in existence centuries past? There only remains to be seen at some future lynching and burning the eating of the roasted victim, and then we shall have reached the *fin de siècle*, the zenith of civilization.

          Arthur A. Schomburg[21]
          New York Times
          June 28, 1903

On May 22, 1902, an African American man named Dudley Morgan was burned at the stake between Longview and Hallsville.

The previous Friday night Morgan and another African American man had reportedly discussed a plan in which Morgan would rob the home of railroad section foreman, J. W. McKee (probably noting that McKee would be at the section house overnight and his wife would be home alone) and they would split the money. In the early hours of Saturday, May 17, Morgan apparently robbed the McKee residence (near the Lansing Switch on the Texas & Pacific Railroad line a few miles east of Hallsville), assaulting Mrs. McKee in the process. Morgan then fled and search parties were formed after sun-up.

Four days later, Morgan was discovered sleeping in ravine approximately seven miles northwest of Mount Vernon. The interim search was little reported and the parties who apprehended Morgan were never identified. The suspect was eventually returned to the scene of the crime by rail.

When the train that Morgan and his captors were aboard reached Marshall at 11 a.m. on May 22, there was already a large crowd at the station and a substantial number of that gathering were there

1902

"Stop" sign along Lansing Switch Rd. between Longview and Hallsville—the area where Dudley Morgan was burned at the stake. *Author's collection.*

to take the train to the Lansing Switch, the location of Morgan's execution (which, by then, was already a foregone conclusion). All the spare coaches in Marshall were brought into service and, at Hallsville, more spectators boarded for the short trip.

The Lansing Switch was not a regular stop on the line between Hallsville and Longview, but an allowance was made for the event. From accounts of the day, locals were beside themselves with anticipation, practically itching for the lynching.

The site for the spectacle was chosen well before Morgan's transport was en route. It was an open space surrounded by trees a quarter of a mile from the switch. A steel railroad track rail had already been driven into the earth to serve as a stake, and, as there were no immediate wells or springs, a lemonade vendor had set up for refreshments.

Several businesses in Longview closed for the event and citizens from Marshall, Longview, Texarkana, Jefferson, Pittsburg, Overton, Kilgore, Beckville, Carthage, etc., had been arriving all morning via every mode of transportation available. The trees that surrounded the site were lined with spectators an hour before the train arrived.

When the transport finally showed up at the switch, the suspect was removed from the opposite side of the train than what the large crowd already there had expected; when the train started to pull out, a dozen Winchester rifles were leveled at the engineer and crew until the misunderstanding was addressed.

After Morgan disembarked, a brakeman ill-advisedly questioned the suspect's guilt and "barely escaped rough handling" by wisely retracting his interrogative.

Morgan's alleged victim, Mrs. McKee, was stationed at the Lansing Switch section house to identify her assailant, and Harrison County sheriff George. W. Munden was present. The newspapers of the day never made clear exactly what Mrs. McKee suffered at the hands of Morgan or what he actually stole or if any of the items or money he took were discovered on his person when he was captured; but when Morgan was brought around, Mrs. McKee (according to the *Dallas Morning News*) succinctly "told them they had the right man and to be calm and burn him to death."

As Sheriff Munden and his men were absurdly outnumbered, the escort conveyed Morgan to the upright rail and affixed him to it. Then, Morgan apparently asked to make a statement.

In his statement, Morgan implicated an accomplice, but also reportedly confessed to the crime. What transpired next was reported differently by the two nearest, major newspapers of the day. The May 23 edition of the *Houston Post* said the victim's husband, J. W. McKee, came forward and applied the torch:

> The wood burned slowly for a while, and the spectators were continually picking at the brute's clothing, trying to tear off pieces for souvenirs. No hot irons were applied to the scorching flesh, but several jabs were made at him with knives and torches passed over his cheeks and breast. Morgan uttered few audible groans and cries. After his clothing had been burned and torn off he begged pitiably to be shot or his death hastened in some manner. Flesh began falling from his body, and it was then very evident that his torture would soon be at an end.

The May 23 edition of the *Dallas Morning News* account differed:

> Morgan confessed to having committed the crime and after being securely chained to the rail with his hands and legs free, the members of the mob began to take ties from a fire already started and burn out his eyes and hold the red-hot and burning timbers to his neck. The negro cringed and let out cries accompanied by the most horrible looks of utter woe and excruciating pain. He was tortured in this slow and painful manner until death came to his relief, the crowd all the while crying "Let him die slow," and the negro begging everyone to shoot him, the tears rolling down his cheeks.

Near the end of the sadistic ritual, an attempt was made to afford Mrs. McKee a proverbial ringside seat, but the carriage she sat in bogged down in the packed crowd and one of the carriage horses reared up, kicking an onlooker in the head.

When Morgan succumbed to the torture, he was unstrapped from the vertical rail and allowed to collapse. The lynch-mob then piled railroad ties over and around his body and prolonged the fire to incinerate him. As soon as the flames died, members of the mob crowded in and poked at the charred carcass with long sticks, fragmenting Morgan's remains. Then, souvenir seekers picked through the ashes for teeth and bits of skull.

Before departing, the crowd raised the two men who captured Morgan high, encouraging them to brandish their weapons while photographers from Marshall, Longview and Hallsville recorded their images for posterity. According to the *Brenham Daily Banner*, the Marshall photographer captured sixteen different shots of Morgan's lynching, but the whereabouts of these images are unknown. The vertical rail utilized for the lynching was left where it stood.

On March 21, 1906, the Campbell and Pilers sawmill (near the Lansing Switch railroad tracks) exploded and the boiler flew 300 yards, landing, rolling and coming to a stop against Morgan's lynch rail, still standing almost four years later.

In mid-October 1902, an African American man named Jim Buchanan was accused of slaying the Hicks family (a husband, wife and daughter) in Nacogdoches County. Buchanan was captured near Henderson (in Rusk County) and Governor Joseph Draper Sayers sent five companies of the state militia to transport him to Nacogdoches.

After taking custody of Buchanan, the militia companies faced a small mob in Henderson and turned it away. They then moved Buchanan to a Rusk jail and encountered would-be vigilantes there as well, so they established a diversionary plan that indicated that they would ship him to Nacogdoches by train. An October 16 headline in the *Southern Mercury* reported that Nacogdoches was "Fixed for a Barbecue" and that preparations had been made to "Roast Jim Buchanan, Negro Murderer."

Lynch-mobs waited at train depots between Rusk and Nacogdoches to seize Buchanan, but the militia contingent clandestinely

Convicted murderer Jim Buchanan was so afraid of being burned by a Nacogdoches mob that he forewent the 30 days allowed to him by law before his execution and was hanged the same day he was found guilty. *Galveston Daily News*, 1902.

transported him by horseback instead. When the militia companies arrived in Nacogdoches with Buchanan, they were met by thousands of infuriated citizens. The armed mob threatened and jeered the escort, but the militia companies calmly and resolutely delivered Buchanan to the Nacogdoches County jailhouse.

The next day Buchanan was tried and convicted by a special term of the district court and sentenced to hang a month hence, on November 17. But outside the frustrated mob had grown so unruly that Buchanan was terrified of being burned alive. He fearfully waived the thirty days allowed to him by law and was hanged that afternoon.

1905

I am an old Confederate soldier. I went through the late Civil War, from the first year to the last year, and it is hardly necessary for me to say that I saw a good deal. I was and am yet a firm believer in the doctrine of State's rights. I am no lover or apologist of the negro. But I am proud that I can say that all the terrors and scenes of that war, coupled with my firm faith in the justice of our cause, did not drive me back to cannibalism, heathenism or barbarism. Our children are in school for good or bad from the cradle to the grave, and early impressions are the most lasting. Now is it possible that thoughtful parents desire, first of all, to stultify the better impulses of their children's natures and cultivate, instead, a spirit of savagery and barbarism? Do they desire them to look with pleasure on the roasting of human beings alive—smile at their haggard countenances and death agonies—horrible, horrible? I freely admit that negroes and others commit crimes for which they ought to speedily die, but not be burned alive.

J. D. Cady
February 1904 letter
to the *Dallas Morning News*
published March 3, 1904

On August 8, 1905, a lynch-mob subdued and imprisoned McLennan County Sheriff G. W. Tilley and his deputies and seized an African American named Sank Majors from the county jail. Majors had been convicted of raping a white woman, but the verdict was tainted by a technical error and Majors was granted a retrial.

A lynch-mob interceded and then split into two groups, one demanding that Majors be burned alive and one saying he should be hanged. The "burning" contingent had gathered packing crates and coal oil and placed them at the base of a telephone pole near city hall, but the "hanging" concern held sway and the mob headed for the Washington Avenue Bridge (over the Brazos River). While en route, however, members of the "burning" faction attempted to defy the hanging advocates. They splashed coal oil on Majors' shirt and ignited it with a tossed match. Members of the hanging faction quickly extinguished the flames, but Majors was seriously burned.

Majors was eventually hanged from the neck at the bridge, and members of the lynch-mob reportedly cut off his fingers as souvenirs.

On August 11, 1905, an African American man named Tom Williams was burned at the stake in Sulphur Springs. That morning, around 6 a.m., a nineteen-year-old white woman named Nettie Griggs was allegedly attacked by a black man who had been following her.

Griggs lived with her sister and brother-in-law, Jacob A. Ellis, on the outskirts of town. She was only 150 yards from the house when the attack supposedly occurred and began screaming immediately. Her sister heard her screams and ran out and helped her back to the house. They immediately contacted the police and search parties were formed.

Sometime around noon, a city marshal named Hall and two private citizens, Wilbur Chaney and Gran Corbin, spotted Tom Williams walking along the Katy Railroad tracks two miles east of town and approximately five miles from the scene of the incident. They took Williams into custody and headed back to the Ellis property for identification.

When the escorting trio and Williams arrived at the Ellis residence, Griggs was suffering from "nervous prostration" and could not face the suspect. A Dr. M. Smith showed up thirty minutes after Williams and his captors and administered an opiate to calm Miss Griggs' nerves. After the drug took effect, Griggs was led to the front door and Williams was presented. According to the *Galveston Daily News* and the *Palestine Daily Herald*, Griggs instantly recognized Williams and said "Yes, that's him; my God, my God, that's him." According to the *Southern Mercury* newspaper, Griggs exclaimed "Take him away and burn him."

By then, a crowd of hundreds was milling around or near the Ellis residence waiting for a positive identification. Once it was made, Williams and his captors headed back to town, the suspect confined to a buggy. The growing mob followed.

When the procession moved within a mile of the courthouse square, Hopkins County Sheriff Jerry Lewis met it and mildly reproached the advocates of a lynching, requesting that the law be allowed to take its course. His plea was ignored.

As the throng verged upon city hall, the editor of the *Sulphur Springs Gazette* approached the buggy that Williams was held in and asked that the suspect be allowed to make a statement. Someone had attempted to chloroform a prominent woman in the community just a few nights before and the journalist thought Williams might be able to shed light on that attack as well.

The journalist's intent was misconstrued and he was "roughly handled." And the procession recommenced.

The mob—whom the *McKinney Democrat* would later refer to as "the best citizens of the county"—was apparently once again accosted by the journalist, but this time he held a rope and claimed that he believed Williams ought to be hung, but not without getting a statement. Stubborn and unrelenting, the throng pressed on.

At the center of the courthouse square, the mob removed Williams from the buggy and doused him in coal oil. He was lit and then "hanged, burning in mid air." When the flames severed the rope and Williams' burning body fell, additional coal oil was applied and this was repeated as necessary until nothing was left except smoldering cinders.

Then, according to the *Democrat*, a prominent African American man named Jim Cherry[22] was "soundly" clubbed for commenting disparagingly of the accuser and told to leave town before sundown (As conveyed in the *Southern Mercury*, an unidentified African American was rendered unconscious by a baseball bat after criticizing the mob as Williams was drug to the stake.).

After the lynching the African American population in Sulphur Springs became "restless" and began exiting the community.

As news of the burning gradually spread, the details were conspicuously exaggerated, presumably to justify the grotesque nature of the execution. The *Southern Mercury* listed Nettie Griggs as a seventeen-year-old and reported that Williams had actually raped her. The *Waxahachie Daily Light* listed Griggs as about fourteen years old and claimed Williams had torn her clothes off. A report in the *Morning Post* (of Raleigh, North Carolina) also identified Griggs as a fourteen-year-old and didn't even bother to veil its bigotry. A subhead read "Texas Mob Makes Quick Work of a Gorilla Negro."

On Friday, September 7, 1905, a twenty-one-year-old African American man named Steve Davis was burned at the stake nine miles southeast of Waxahachie.

Three days prior, on September 4, Mrs. S. P. Norris was attacked in her home near Howard, a small farming community five miles south of Lake Waxahachie. Mr. and Mrs. Norris had a newborn/infant child and, on the day of the attack, the child was asleep in a cradle next to their bed. Mr. Norris was out and Mrs. Norris was sitting next to the cradle. The assailant entered the residence, crept up behind Mrs. Norris and punched her in the back of the head. He then reportedly struck her in the face four times and fled (Some reports indicated that the suspect "pulled out" the victim's tongue as well, but as she gave verbal testimony repeatedly in the days after the attack, this claim was obviously exaggerated.).

Though Mrs. Norris was struck first from behind, subject to a blow that may or may not have rendered her unconscious (or semi-lucid)—and possibly unable to identify her assailant, much less determine his ethnicity—on Wednesday, September 6, an African American named Tom Wiley was arrested for her assault in Blooming Grove (Navarro County). Wiley was able to demonstrate his innocence and released.

Ellis County Sheriff Joe P. Minnick and a legion of concerned citizens had made inquiries regarding a few African Americans besides Wiley, reportedly presenting some of the suspects to Mrs. Norris; but none appeared to be her attacker and investigators were (as the *Waxahachie Daily Light* phrased it) "almost at sea," with few clues and less leads. At some point in the process, however, the assault charge was trumped up to a rape claim, and the investigation picked up steam.

Steve Davis lived alone in the area (near "Maloney" or "Maloney's farm," where he worked) and had picked cotton for Mr. Norris in the past. As the investigation lagged, two to three white men from Howard began observing Davis's cabin. When word circulated that Davis was planning on leaving Maloney—possibly due to his white neighbors' probably conspicuous suspicions or the increasingly heated search for a lone, guilty black man—he was taken into civilian custody and transported to an old tenant house in a grove near the Norris home.

Davis's civilian captors kept him under "strong" guard and grilled him most of the day. The amateur sleuths described him as sullen and uncooperative early on, but claimed that by the afternoon he had made a partial confession.

Davis quickly retracted his partial confession possibly because he realized a false admission wasn't going to do him any good.

Davis' captors had located him in close proximity to the Norris residence with the intention of taking him to Mrs. Norris for identification. It was subsequently decided that Mrs. Norris—like Miss Griggs—should be medicated before Davis was presented, and Dr. F. H. Jenkins was contacted. He arrived directly and administered an opiate.

By early afternoon word had spread that a promising suspect was in custody for the outrage against the Norris family which, again, had evolved from a matter of blows to a full-blown sexual assault.

White citizens from Waxahachie, Italy, Milford, etc., began leaving work and heading to Howard. Sheriff Minnick also made a beeline for the proceeding, but when he got there he was outnumbered and could only attempt to positively (or lawfully) impact the events as best he could. When Davis was presented to Mrs. Norris, she said she was not sure he was the perpetrator. Sheriff Minnick subsequently asked that he be permitted to take charge of the suspect until his guilt could be established.

While the sheriff and the civilian contingent were debating this option, Davis was stripped by his captors and they observed what looked like scratches on his person. As Mrs. Norris had been reportedly waylaid from behind and suffered repeated blows to the face after, the inference that she scratched her attacker or that the scratches would have remained (or could have comprised plausible evidence) four days after the attack was obviously weak. It was also entirely plausible that the "scratches" might have had other origins, the most obvious of which were Davis's civilian seizure and possible forced partial confession. But, as detailed in previous chapters, anything that could be propounded regarding the guilt of a black man usually was.

Once Davis was stripped, he was again presented to Mrs. Norris and this time she positively identified him as her attacker. Remanding Davis to Sheriff Minnick's custody was no longer an option.

After Mrs. Norris identified Davis as the perpetrator, however, she made a curious request: she asked that he be hanged and not burned. Her appeal was communicated to the growing throng of vigilantes and initially approved, many obviously interested in respecting the victim's wishes. But an element in the body civic was not comfortable with the suggestion, almost as if it would be anticlimactic, especially in terms of the gathering crowd. These contrarians formed a committee that revisited Mrs. Norris and apparently badgered her. In the end, she reportedly remarked that she didn't care what happened to Davis and said "You may burn him for a day and a half for all I care."

By 5 p.m., the throng had become a mob. According to an on-hand reporter for the *Daily Light*, "It seemed that the people came up out of the earth, the crowd increased in size so rapidly, and when the execution took place it was estimated that more than three thousand were on the ground."

When the committee announced Mrs. Norris' change of heart, cheers were heard all around and the next order of business became logistics. The lynching had been planned for 7 p.m., but leaders of the mob decided to postpone the conflagration for one hour to allow anyone who wanted to witness the event extra time to arrive. Then there was the issue of location, and this was put to a vote.

The leading options were a grassland depression or a nearby meadow. The meadow carried the voting, but the crowd learned that the individual in charge of the meadow was a renter and he asked that the lynching be moved. The affair was relocated to the depression in the corner of a field.

After location concerns were addressed, the vigilantes turned their attentions towards wood for the fire and stake construction. A local farmer named Jordan Brown donated a nearby dilapidated barn and members of the mob dismantled it and chopped the lumber up for kindling. The stake was comprised of two large, 10-foot-long iron pipes, driven into the ground a body's width apart and bound together up top by wire and chain.

During the interlude between Mrs. Norris' positive identification of Davis as the suspect and the preparations for the lynching,

1905

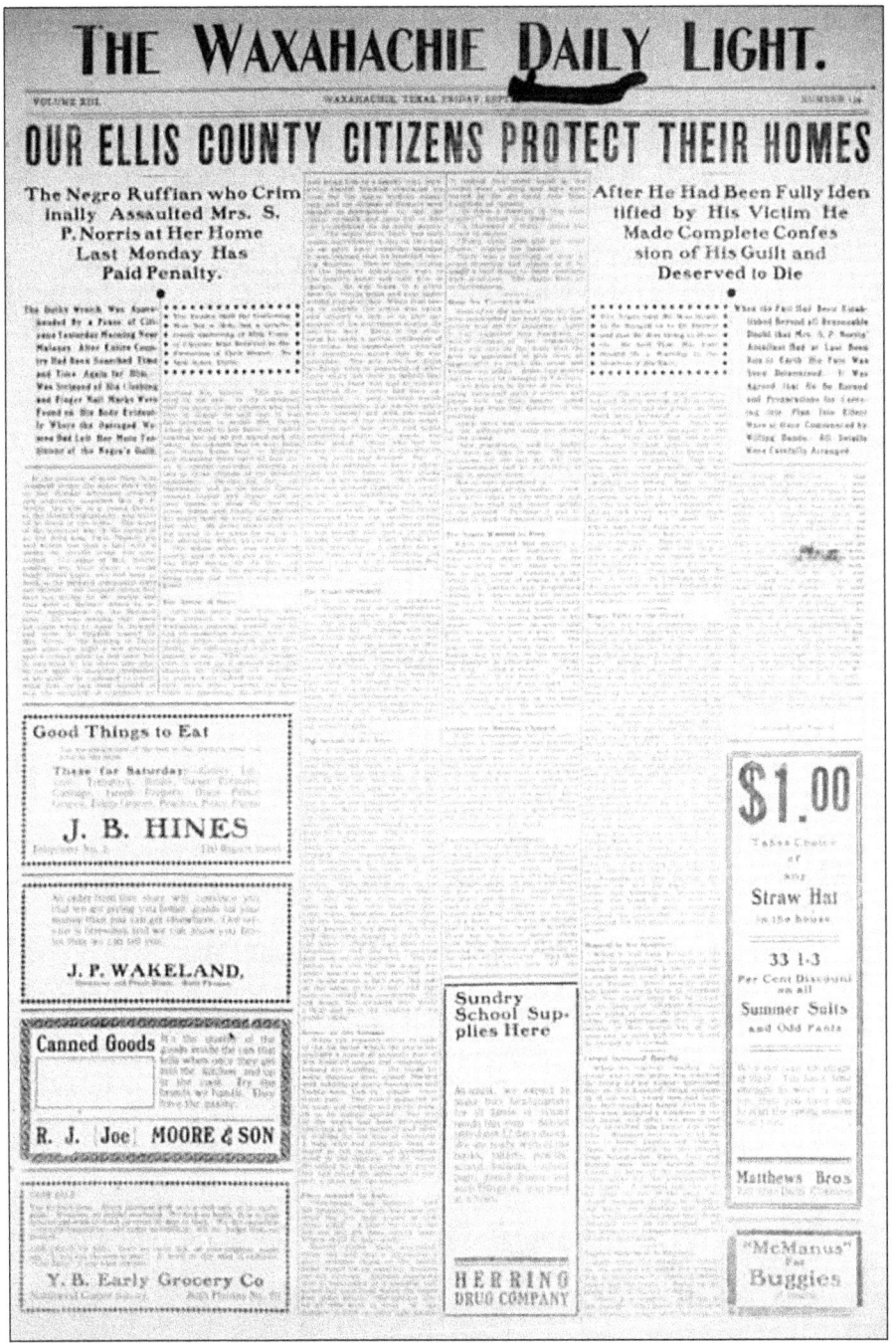

The justification for the burning of the "Negro Ruffian" Steve Davis took up the *Waxahachie Daily Light's* entire front page. *Waxahachie Daily Light*, 1905.

Davis reportedly voided his retraction and re-confessed (the *Daily Light* reporter was there to record it):

> I slipped up behind her and struck her on the side of the head with my fist. I hit her four or five times in the face. I struck heavy blows. She fell off the bed and onto the floor and I got scared and run. I did not commit criminal [sexual] assault on her.

Realizing his death was inevitable, Davis' re-confession was possibly proffered falsely to reiterate the point that no sexual assault had been involved and in hopes of avoiding the torch. This calculation was fruitless. His fate was already sealed.

As the lynching stake was completed, a murmur began to circulate suggesting that after Davis's punishment was dispensed, the assembly ought to make its way to the Waxahachie jail and lynch another African American man named Albert Johnson. Johnson was awaiting trial for the murder of a white man named J. H. Taylor. The proposition was popular and the leaders of the mob once again called for a vote. The recommendation was affirmed by a large majority and Sheriff Minnick immediately rushed to Waxahachie to relocate Johnson.

The *Daily Light* later melodramatically conveyed the mob's unanimity and collective sense of righteousness as the proceeding approached it final moments:

> Young men and old men, men who had years ago fought under the Stars and Bars, as well as those who fought under the Stars and Stripes, were determined to mete out justice to the vile culprit who had violated the sanctity of a home. There was no thought that the military would interfere. There was no fear of special trains from Dallas, Waco or other points bearing the uniformed guardians of the peace of the country. Had they come, it would have been all the same. The people of that enterprising and thrifty section of Ellis County were aroused and no power on earth could have prevented or stayed the execution of Steve Davis.

When all the preparations were made, one of the lynch-mob's ringleaders addressed the group:

> This is no mob. This is a gathering of gentlemanly citizens of Ellis County who believe in the protection of their wives and daughters by making examples of black brutes who violate the sanctity of a home. There's no mob spirit here, it is a spirit of

justice that prevails. If there is a white man here who endorses the crime of this negro let him suffer the same fate. Let everyone sit down and keep quiet during these proceedings. We are not here to gloat over this affair and everybody should refrain from applauding after the torch has been applied.

Before Davis was affixed to the stake, he asked to pray and his request was granted. He began to pray silently but a voice from the throng demanded he pray out loud; the antagonist was shouted down by his fellows.

As Davis was ushered to the stake, he reportedly reiterated his guilt, but denied the charge of sexual assault. He also apparently said that he knew he was going to heaven regardless of the manner of his death.

While two men held Davis aloft at the stake, two others fastened him to the high end of the pipes, suspending him a few feet above the ground and within full view of the crowd (which eventually included many women and children). His hands were secured behind him but his feet remained untethered.

Mr. Norris was summoned to apply the torch and then the conflagration began. The *Daily Light* waxed poetic and dramatic and then became graphic:

> The scene was indeed weird and beggared description. The moon passed behind a cloud and a sky of inky blackness, now and then illuminated by fitful flashes of lightning, intoned by low peals of thunder, formed a fit setting for the tragedy. More fuel and more oil were added to the fire, increasing the volume of the flames. The negroes shoes had been removed and as the flames began to singe his feet and lower limbs his struggles began. He kicked this way and that to keep his feet from the seething flames which were increasing all the time, but all efforts to escape the fiery ordeal were wasted energy. He never groaned but one time, and as the flames would shoot above his head he would gasp at them in an effort to swallow them, thus hoping to quickly end his suffering. His pants soon caught fire and gradually the blaze ate its way around his body. The fire was allowed to burn him slowly at first in order that he might suffer all the tortures possible, but when the flames began enveloping his body life was soon extinct. Soon his lower limbs became rigid and blood began to stream from his mouth, making the scene almost too ghastly to be described. After the body had been burned to a crisp it was lowered into the bonfire and when the blaze was finally extin-

guished nothing but a smoldering heap of ashes remained.

Excepting ads, the *Daily Light's* coverage of the Davis lynching would take up the entire September 8 front page and generally baptize the lawlessness rather than bemoan it. Trumpeting the obviously tenuous supposition that Davis was a "rape fiend" and stressing that the lynch-mob was "quiet and orderly," the reporting proclaimed the lynch-mob representative of a citizenship that was a credit to the region and "true to the core" and remarked that "When Ellis County does a thing she does it in regular form."

According to the *New York Times*, Davis's ashes were gathered up by his brother and sister, both of whom lived in Palmer. Some reports suggest that at Davis's request members of the mob attempted to contact them before the lynching, but they could not be reached or were reached and arrived late.

On September 12, an African American known as Long Jim reportedly received 100 lashes on his bare back from the citizens of Mansfield for suggesting that Mrs. Norris might have been agreeable to Davis's advances. Jim was also ordered to make himself scarce and never return.

On September 28, 1905, a white woman named Lora Conditt, her twelve-year-old daughter Mildred and her sons Herschell, Jesse and Joseph were bludgeoned and hacked to death in their Edna, Texas home. The mother and daughter had also been sexually assaulted and the incident received intense statewide coverage.

The murders were initially reported by an African American teenager named Monk Gibson, who had been in the Conditt family's employ. Gibson was subsequently suspicioned and taken into custody, and local white vigilantes almost immediately began making arrangements to burn him at the stake. On September 30, Gibson escaped while being transferred to Hallettsville.

Gibson remained at large for almost two weeks but his family was arrested and jailed in his stead. A portion of the townspeople felt that they might have assisted in Monk's escape and sheriff's department officials were weary of a mob burning the Gibson family in Monk's place. Some elements of the community even suspected that Gibson hadn't actually escaped at all and that members of local law enforcement were hiding him. Governor Samuel W. T. Lanham sent militia companies from Austin and Houston to Edna to maintain order and prevent the Gibson family from facing the torch, and Monk was recaptured on October 9.

After a change of venue, Gibson's first trial in Bexar County resulted in a mistrial; his second, closer to Edna (in adjacent DeWitt County), resulted in a guilty verdict. Though his guilt was arguably never satisfactorily established, attempts to appeal his conviction were unsuccessful, and he was hanged in front of a large crowd in Cuero on June 27, 1908.

The occasion that a black man implicated in the rape and murder of two white females even made it to trial was considered a landmark accomplishment in the annals of Texas justice.

1908

Four thousand persons have been put to death without warrant of law in the United States in the last quarter of a century. Ninety-five percent of them were negroes charged with assaults on white women. The methods of execution comprised hanging, shooting, flogging, burning at the stake and flaying... Burning at the stake has been almost as frequent as hanging, and more frequent than shooting. The example was set by the people of Paris, Tex, in February, 1893, when Henry Smith, a negro farmhand, was burned alive after he had been tortured with red-hot irons.

Fort Wayne Sentinel
September 26, 1906

On July 28, 1908, an eighteen-year-old African American man named Ted Smith was burned at the stake in Greenville.

Smith and his family worked as laborers for a white man named R. H. Delancey on his farm near Clinton, just eight miles southwest of Greenville, in Hunt County. According to oral accounts, a relationship sprang up between Smith and Delancey's fifteen-year-old daughter, Viola, and they carried on in secret. When Viola's parents discovered the dangerous courtship, they apparently pretended to be unaware until they could catch the two and cry foul.

On July 26, a circumstance presented itself and Mr. and Mrs. Delancey had Smith charged with criminal assault. Smith fled and law enforcement personnel and groups of enraged citizens set out in pursuit.

On July 27, Smith was spotted in the Caddo Creek bottoms near Clinton, but managed to escape. When Smith was later captured by two police officers at a nearby farm around dusk, he was quietly picking a banjo and insisted he had done nothing wrong.

Smith's captors correctly assumed that their chances of avoiding

1908

The "Negro Smith" was later found to be innocent of all charges, save being romantically involved with a young white woman. *Courtesy of Texas State Library & Archives Commission.*

the roving bands of would-be vigilantes while en route to the county jail would be slim. They decided to take Smith deeper into the backwoods and lay low. Their decision was prescient. By 6 p.m. the returning search parties had formed a mob outside the county jail and were milling around the public square, eager for news.

Both Hunt County Sheriff David L. Hemsell and District Judge T. D. Montrose addressed the unruly crowd and eventually it dispersed. The two police captors and Smith eluded the mobs for several hours and Smith was delivered to the county jail in Greenville at approximately 3:30 a.m. on July 28. By 8 a.m. the mob had returned.

Sheriff Hemsell reappeared and explained to the mob that he had to convey the prisoner to the victim's house so he could be identified. Spokespersons for the mob promised safe conduct for Sheriff Hemsell and Smith to the Delancey household and back, so the sheriff commandeered a buggy and headed towards Clinton with the suspect.

When Smith was presented to Viola for identification, she said "That is the nigger that did the deed." Smith cried out in shock and Sheriff Hemsell turned the buggy back towards town.

Once back in Greenville, Sheriff Hemsell was set upon by the waiting mob and relieved of his suspect.

First the mob took Smith to the north corner of the public square, where members placed a rope around his neck and started to hang him. Then, as McKinney's *Weekly Democrat-Gazette* put it, "other heads prevailed for a more impressive death, so it was decided to burn him." The crowd dragged Smith to the south side of the town square by the rope around his neck and placed him on a cord of wood. He was then doused with coal oil and incinerated in front of 1,000 people.

As Smith burned, an older African American in the crowd remarked that the whole ordeal was unfortunate and he was immediately horsewhipped.

When pressed for an official response to the broad daylight lynching of Ted Smith, Greenville Mayor Joseph F. Nichols relegated it to the ledger of business as usual:

> There will be no action taken by the authorities of Greenville relative to the burning of the rapist this morning. The deed was committed by the negro and the penalty of death was administered by an orderly body of the citizens from the city and the country. The negro was properly identified and taken from the sheriff and the incident is closed as far as the city is concerned.

Mayor Nichols' proclamation was popularly received, the *West Texas News* (out of Colorado City, Texas) noting that "the signal revenge of the Greenville citizens has brought praise from every portion of the state and may furnish a good object lesson for other would be assaulters."

The *Democrat-Gazette's* conclusions were less complimentary, but granted Greenville an exception because there was "no parallel in the history of the state to this case, possibly, with the exception of the Paris case."

Viola Delancey later recanted and Sheriff Hemsell himself eventually admitted that he thought Smith had been innocent. No one involved in the lynching was ever charged or prosecuted, and two of the lynch-mob ringleaders later reportedly rose to the public offices of Hunt County sheriff and Greenville fire chief.

Not long after the Ted Smith burning, the town of Greenville would embrace another controversial civic act "administered by an

1908

The broad daylight, public square lynching of Ted Smith was a community affair in Greenville, home of the "Blackest Land" and "The Whitest People."
Courtesy of Texas State Library & Archives Commission.

orderly body" of its citizens. It adopted a new community slogan and celebrated it on a large banner that hung across main street. It proclaimed: "Welcome to Greenville: The Blackest Land and the Whitest People." It would greet Greenville visitors for decades.

1909

There have been some indignant protests in the North against an occasional Southern habit of lynching by fire. Such protests are folly, as is to a large extent all criticism of Southern lynching. Difference in latitude makes little difference in human nature. A mob's a mob no matter what the state. . . A lynching is a lynching, bad always and everywhere.

Houston Post
November 2, 1909

On March 7, 1909, an African American man named Anderson Ellis was burned at the stake in Rockwall, Texas.

According to reports, Ellis was laboring under the employ of a white man named Arthur McKinney, at McKinney's farm five miles east of town, near Fate, Texas. On Friday, March 5, McKinney left early on a business trip to Royce City (a few miles northeast). Shortly after her husband left, Mrs. McKinney reportedly stepped into the back yard and was seized by Ellis, who allegedly attempted to "criminally assault" her.

Though Ellis was described as being a stout man, almost six feet tall and weighing 180 pounds, Mrs. McKinney supposedly escaped his grasp and fled back into the house. Then (according to the *Palestine Daily Herald*), "Closing the door, she looked through the window and saw the negro running away, menacing her and calling that he would murder her should she reveal his attempted act."

News of the alleged assault, "menacing" and parting threat spread quickly and white men (and boys) from all over the area armed themselves and joined in the search for Ellis. For close to two days the search parties had no luck and then, at around 4 a.m. Sunday morning, a group approached the farmhouse of an African American named Andrew Clark.

The searchers requested permission to examine Clark's residence and Clark refused to give it. As members of the search party began to make demands, two African American men fled from the rear of the residence and were immediately fired upon. Clark's son Will was killed instantly and Ellis got away. The search party utilized bloodhounds to track the fugitive.

By 8 a.m. the searchers had located Ellis at the farmhouse of J. R. Harper, three miles south of Caddo Mills. Ellis was trapped but apparently armed. A short gun battle ensued, the suspect hitting no one, but receiving a couple of bullet wounds himself. After he ran out of ammunition the search party disarmed him and took him into custody.

Ellis was transported to Caddo Mills and handed over to Constable George B. Dugan. Dugan mustered a few automobiles and transferred Ellis to the Hunt County jail in Greenville, delivering him at 10:30 a.m. Ellis received medical attention at the jail.

Once word got around that Ellis had been captured, mobs began forming in Greenville and the surrounding towns. Though Greenville was only seven months removed from the burning of Ted Smith, authorities there sought evasive measures and transferred Ellis thirteen miles northwest to the small community of Celeste. At Celeste, Ellis was placed on a passenger train to Dallas and, in Dallas, was handed over to Sheriff Hall of Rockwall County.

Sheriff Hall and Ellis boarded a passenger train to Rockwall and arrived there just before 10 p.m. Ellis was placed in the Rockwall County jail, but his incarceration was short-lived. Within minutes a mob appeared at the jail, overpowered the authorities and seized Ellis, transferring him one last time to a large iron rail that had been driven into the earth downtown. According to the *Dallas Morning News*, the mob was all business:

> There was no rowdyism permitted. The leaders of the mob, whose names are not known to your correspondent, gave out that any attempt to thwart the will of the crowd would meet with summary vengeance.

By 11 p.m., Ellis was tied to the rail and kerosene-soaked timber was piled up around him. Some reports alleged that he had earlier confessed, but at the stake he refused to make a statement. The kindling was lit and Ellis was rapidly consumed by the flames. He remained unsettlingly silent and composed throughout.

Black Holocaust

Anderson Ellis was burned at the stake in Rockwall for allegedly attacking the wife of his employer, Arthur McKinney. *Daily Bulletin*, 1909.

Garland coroner W. F. Bane would later confirm that Will Clark was killed by gunshot wounds, but his murder would never receive an investigation.

While Ellis was being tracked earlier that Sunday, Collin County Sheriff George M. Eubank mistook an African American man named Dennis Frazier for Ellis and arrested him on a local train. Sheriff Eubank escorted Frazier to a McKinney jail and, after discovering his mistake, charged Frazier with "unlawfully riding a train" instead. On March 8, Frazier plead guilty to hitching a ride on a train and was fined $15, which the *McKinney Courier-Gazette* noted he would likely be working off in county highway maintenance efforts.

Just below this mention, the *Courier-Gazette* reported that an African American named Rasho Tucker had also been arrested (by Collin County Deputy Sheriff Albert McCauley) for the assault of a black woman named Mary Johnson. As the penalty for assaulting a black woman was a minor offense, Tucker plead guilty and was fined $13.70.[23]

1910

Why are there so many lynchings? Because the law does not attend to its business properly. If our people could rely on summary justice being meted out to murderers and their like, there would be no need for lynchings and there would be none.

Greenville Morning Herald
December 7, 1910

On June 20, 1910, an African American man named Leonard Johnson was burned at the stake in Cherokee County.

Earlier that day, a seventeen-year-old white girl named Maude Redden was found in a clump of bushes near the town of Lone Star, thirteen miles northeast of Rusk. Her throat was reportedly slit from ear-to-ear and her body was bruised and lacerated.

Maude's father (W. H. Redden, a Lone Star constable) and brother had gone to Rusk for a meeting of the local Democratic Executive Committee on the day of the attack and an African American convict named Leonard Johnson was left working off a fine on the Redden property, doing plow work. Maude had left the Redden place for the customary one-and-a-half mile walk to her 1 p.m. music lesson in Lone Star and had neither arrived nor returned.

When Maude's body was discovered, Cherokee County Sheriff C. K. "Knox" Norwood and ten deputies traveled to Lone Star and, as the *Palestine Daily Herald* put it, Johnson—though not having fled—was "immediately suspicioned and arrested."

Johnson "stoutly" proclaimed his innocence, but Sheriff Norwood took him into custody and headed to the county jail in Rusk. A few miles outside of town, the sheriff and his men were confronted by an angry, white mob (of approximately 150 men) that quickly encircled and overpowered them and seized Johnson. Then, a number

1910

Allen Brooks was pulled out of a second floor window of the Dallas County Courthouse and then drug to a street corner and hanged from a telephone pole. Dallas Police chief John Ryan cut Brooks' body down before a Dallas mob could burn it. *From the collections of the Texas/Dallas History Archives Division of the Dallas Public Library.*

of outraged African Americans in the area appeared and attempted to liberate Johnson from the white mob; but they, too, were outnumbered and beaten back.

The mob tortured Johnson until he confessed and then hung him and shot him, leaving enough life in him to suffer being burned at the stake. Then, they piled the available brush high and applied the torch.

The next day the entire Lone Star community showed up for Maude Redden's funeral and Johnson's ashes were either raked into a pauper's grave or left to drift in the wind. A sympathizer mourned Miss Redden's untimely passing in the *Daily Herald*, deploring "the dumb fright she must have experienced when confronted by the beast" and noting that it was "evident that the negro is the curse of this nation."

Sheriff Norwood later stated that not a single person in the lynching party was recognizable to he or his deputies and his office would not be undertaking efforts to identify Johnson's executioners.

One month later, on July 22, 1910, an eighteen-year-old African American named Henry Gentry was burned at the stake in Belton.

On July 21, a black man was allegedly seen looking into the window of the home of a white widow named Mrs. Lamb, who lived with her daughter. The daughter reportedly fired a gun at the unfamiliar black face and the figure fled.

Lamb's neighbors called local Constable Jim Mitchell and he came over to investigate. Mitchell had no suspects, but did find a pair of shoes and a hat beneath a window.

At this point, Constable Mitchell left and procured bloodhounds to take the scent of the hat and shoes and track down the culprit. But when he returned, he was shot in the back by someone behind a tree.

Though he died within minutes of being shot in the back by a figure behind a tree, Mitchell apparently still managed to recognize his killer and identified him as Gentry. When additional officers and concerned citizens took charge of the bloodhounds and attempted to put them on the scent of Gentry from the hat and shoes, the hounds were disinclined to leave the Lamb house. As the *Dallas Morning News* put it, the "hounds would not trail the negro."

Disregarding the possibility that the hat and shoes might have belonged to someone at the Lamb residence (and thus explaining why the hounds refused to leave), search parties were sent out in every direction the next morning. Gentry was spotted in a large spread of tall Johnson grass next to a cornfield three miles from Belton. Reports of the sighting neglected to mention Gentry minus his shoes or hat.

The searchers converged on the prairie and filled the tall grass with shot, but Gentry didn't emerge. All available automobiles were utilized to send for additional help.

Eventually, Bell County Sheriff David C. Burkes and 500 concerned citizens surrounded the area en masse and closed in slowly. About halfway in, they spotted Gentry and requested he surrender. When Gentry refused, he was shot twice and reportedly reconsidered.

A citizen subsequently placed a rope around Gentry's neck and he was dragged into the open and placed in an automobile.

As Constable Mitchell had been a popular public servant, Gentry's fate was decided well before he was captured. A spot in the

Henry Gentry was shot, dragged and burned at the stake in Belton on July 22, 1910, and the *Daily Telegram* apparently reported the lynching *in media res*. *Temple Daily Telegram*, 1910.

public square of Belton had already been stocked with wood and coal oil and hundreds if not thousands waited.

When Gentry was delivered to the town square, he was apparently stripped and another rope was placed around his neck. This rope was attached to a horse and Gentry was dragged around the square at full gallop and then cut loose next to the spot of his execution. An "insensate" Gentry was then "consigned to the flames until totally destroyed."

In the midst of the conflagration a large portion of the onlookers began demanding that Gentry's brother and another African American—who had been with Gentry at some point the night before and were being held as witnesses—be lynched as well. The ambitious crowd started for the Bell County jail.

Sheriff Burkes met the mob at the jail and stood up to the ringleaders, and then he and Judge A. L. Curtis (a cousin of the dead constable) implored the crowd to cease and desist. The crowd was unmoved, but Judge H. B. Savage joined Curtis and between the three they temporarily averted further mayhem. Later, a plan to storm the county jail was proposed, but District Judge John Robinson addressed the aspirants and Sheriff Burke had the prisoners in question secretly removed and transferred.

The *Temple Daily Telegram's* final reporting on the lynching included a special sidebar referring to the Gentry family as a "den of criminals" that had cost Bell County a small fortune in prosecutions and punishments, clearly suggesting that Henry Gentry's lynching had saved the taxpayers lots of money.

On November 3, 1910, a twenty-year-old Mexican ranch hand named Antonio Rodriquez was burned at the stake in Rock Springs, Texas.

Rodriquez, of Las Vacas, Mexico, was accused of shooting Mrs. Lem Henderson to death at her home on the outskirts of town and subsequently arrested nine miles farther out. He was placed in the Rock Springs jail but later seized when local vigilantes stormed the dilapidated facility.

The vigilante force transported Rodriquez to a pre-prepared execution pyre and there he allegedly confessed, claiming he killed Mrs. Henderson because she "spoke mean" to him. The lynch-mob

1910

put him to the torch and he reportedly died stoically. The coroner's verdict simply stated that "an unknown Mexican was burned by unknown parties" and no local investigation of the incident commenced.

News of the lynching spread and, within a week, Mexicans were rioting in protest across Eastern Mexico, stoning American travelers and vandalizing the home of the U. S. Consul. On November 9, Mexican Ambassador Francisco León De La Barra[24] presented a claim for reparation to the U. S. State Department and was assured a full investigation would be conducted. On November 11, the Mexican government cancelled all bullfights in Mexico to guard against further anti-American outbursts. By November 12, all the Texas Rangers in the area were mustered and massed at strategic points along the border to intercept anticipated retaliatory raids from Mexican mobs.

A stereotypical depiction of Antonio Rodriguez's lynching near Rock Springs. *Donaldsonville Chief,* 1910.

The U. S. State Department instructed Texas Governor Thomas Campbell to look into the situation and Campbell, in turn, pressured Edwards County to investigate. On December 15, a Rock Springs grand jury began reviewing the lynching, but concluded its proceedings just before Christmas and rendered no indictments.

Before the affair came to a head, the Mexican Revolution commenced and Mexico descended into chaos.[25]

1912

> Historical truth, as defined and dictated by the Confederate societies, insured that Southerners would retain cultural values ultimately detrimental to the progress of their own native land.
> **Fred Arthur Bailey**
> "Free Speech and the 'Lost Cause' in Texas: A Study of Social Control in the South,"
> *Southwestern Historical Quarterly*
> **January 1994**

On May 25, 1912 a second African American man was burned at the stake in Tyler. His name was Dan Davis.

On May 13, 1912, a sixteen-year-old white girl named Carrie Johnson was attacked along the railroad tracks just outside of Tyler at approximately 2:30 p.m. Her assailants reportedly "criminally assaulted" her, knocked out some of her teeth, partially crushed her skull and then cut her throat and left her for dead.

Johnson survived, her attackers' knives apparently narrowly missing her jugular vein. She was discovered the next morning around 6 a.m., supposedly clinging to life.

Johnson hadn't known or recognized her assailants, but an unidentified man apparently saw a black man in the general vicinity at some point before or after the assault. Based on this unsubstantiated, imprecise information, a circular was created by a Tyler police officer and disseminated around the state. The circular found itself in the hands of Henry Burch, a farmer who lived near Powell, seventy miles to the northwest. Davis had been doing work for Burch, and Burch thought he resembled the suspect portrayed in the Tyler circular.

On May 24, Burch got a car, solicited the help of three Powell-area citizens and seized Davis. He then relayed the capture to Tyler officials and began driving to Athens. Meanwhile, a seventy-five person Tyler contingent caught the first train to Athens.

The Athens authorities took control of Davis but were confronted by the Tyler concern and 200 locals who believed Davis should be returned to Tyler for identification. Athens authorities relinquished custody of Davis after the Tyler constituency assured them that Davis would not be "molested" until his guilt was established.

The Tyler contingent (along with eighty residents of Athens) arrived home with the suspect in tow at 1:42 a.m. and Carrie Johnson was sent for to provide identification. A mob 1,000 strong met Davis and his escort at the train depot and another crowd formed at the public square.

Tyler law enforcement personnel addressed the growing mob at the railroad station, requesting that no action be taken until the identification of the suspect had been established. The mob acquiesced, but followed the Tyler authorities and the prisoner to the county jail.

As the procession passed the public square the prospect of lynching Davis was straightaway revisited, but, by then the victim's father had joined the escort and entreated the crowd to stay its hand until his daughter arrived and confirmed the suspect's guilt.

The procession made it to the county jail and while the mob waited for Johnson to arrive, the authorities apparently questioned Davis. According to the *Dallas Morning News*, Davis "broke down under the constant fire" of his interrogators and implicated an accomplice who was currently being held in a Waco jail. Davis reportedly claimed his confederate was responsible for the attempted throat-slitting but admitted to striking Johnson in the face with a railroad spike, "stunning her so that she could make no resistance."

The instant that Davis' confession was recorded, preparations for his lynching accelerated. The anxious mob decided that his coerced admission was enough and that a positive identification was unnecessary. Tyler law enforcement personnel objected, but they were vastly outnumbered and their protests proved futile.

At 4 a.m., May 25, Davis was bound to a steel rail in the public square and various combustibles were stacked beneath and around him. As a crowd of 2,000 looked on, he allegedly reiterated his confession and then a torch was applied. The rising flames consumed him in twenty minutes, but not before he supposedly begged his executioners to cut his throat with a razor.

The *El Paso Herald* noted that "the work of the lynchers was done quickly and quietly," the deed seemingly having "a sobering effect upon them." But it didn't prevent 200-300 concerned Smith County vigilantes from departing for Waco in two separate attempts to retrieve Davis' alleged accomplice, whom the May 26 edition of the *Washington Post* identified as George A. Price.

In the May 27 edition the *Post*, reports indicated that Price had been safely transported to a penitentiary in Rusk, but Rusk officials refused to confirm or deny the claim. The same edition of the *Bryan Daily Eagle and Pilot* reported that McLennan County Deputy Sheriff Phil Hobbs had actually delivered Price to the Bexar County jail in San Antonio.

In mid-June, Price was officially released from the Bexar County jail after a possible indictment against him in the Carrie Johnson assault case was no-billed by a Tyler grand jury. Instead of returning to the Tyler or Waco areas, Price chose to remain in the Bexar County jail as an employee of the state.

In 1998, in his otherwise comprehensive *Born In Dixie: The History of Smith County, Texas* (Eakin Press), author James Smallwood noted the broad-daylight 1909 lynching of an innocent African American man named Jim Hodges[26] as an instance illustrative of the brutality blacks endured in the Tyler area in the early 20th century and the resultant "negative image" that Smith County suffered due to the incident, but conspicuously disincluded accounts of the public burnings of Dan Davis and Henry Hillard, both of which obviously contributed just as much (if not more) to the community's disquieting reputation.[27]

1915

No county in Texas can boast of better citizenship than can the good county of Bell. What the citizens did on this occasion has been done by citizens of a number of counties in Texas, and will be done by many others throughout the State in the future, if occasion demands, and no power or law on earth can prevent it... Public sentiment endorsed the action of the people of Paris, Tyler and Corsicana when they applied the torch to the negro brutes for unspeakable crimes. That accounts for the fact that no conviction has ever been secured in cases of this kind. Public sentiment endorsed the action of the good people of Bell County and no indictment will ever be found against any man who participated in the burning of Stanley. It is a closed incident.

Cameron Herald
August 12, 1915

On July 31, 1915, a thirty-one-year-old African American man named Will Stanley was burned at the stake in Temple, Texas,

The previous Wednesday night someone broke into the home of William R. Grimes and, armed with a railroad track hammer, beat him and his wife senseless and murdered three of his children. The next day, when a neighbor paid a visit to the residence (which was on the southeast outskirts of the city), five-year-old Marguerite Grimes opened their door to reveal the carnage. According to the *Lancaster Herald*:

> On one bed in the room lay the inanimate form of Mrs. Grimes, her face beaten to a jelly, the body covered with blood, the woman unconscious and groaning in pain. On a bed in another part of the room reposed the form of the husband with his skull crushed and other fearful injuries in evidence. On a cot lay the body of Willie Grimes, a son of 7, a gory spectacle and a pitiable object, with the little skull mashed in, the features obliterated and cuts and

gashes covering the entire body. Further investigation showed that the twin infants of the couple, Frank and Mary Grimes, aged 7 months, had been murdered while in the bed with the mother, the little heads also being crushed in. The distorted, twisted bodies of the little victims presented a most horrifying spectacle.

Three other children, including Marguerite, had been asleep in a separate room that the perpetrator(s) left undisturbed.

Mr. and Mrs. Grimes were hospitalized and Marguerite and the two other surviving children were taken in by A. L. Flint, a friend of the family.

On July 29, Texas Governor James E. Ferguson (a native of Bell County), Bell County Sheriff Hugh Smith and relatives of the Grimes family offered a $1,700 reward for the capture of the guilty party in the Grimes family assault and murders.

On Friday, July 30, Stanley was arrested in Rogers (fifteen miles southeast of Temple) after he was spotted wearing a pair of trousers marked with the name "W. R. Grimes." Stanley told the arresting officers (Rogers City Marshall Albert Bonds and Constable Logan Parks) that he had no knowledge of the Grimes murders and claimed that he had gotten the trousers from two other African American men, Rodell "Slim" Harrison of Fort Worth (identified in some newspapers as Claude J. Harris) and Dicey Wells of Temple (identified in some newspapers as Dicey Bell). They had met early that morning in Temple and were all making their way to Rogers where Stanley planned to work at the railroad section house.

County law enforcement officers took Stanley into custody and headed for Belton, the Bell County seat. Their car broke down a few miles short and, since word of a black suspect in custody had spread, they thought it best to get off the main roads. They took to the woods around Little River and attempted to wait out possible vigilante traffic. When the searching vigilantes became aware of their detour, they surrounded the woody area along Little River and the officers surrendered with their prisoner.

The law enforcement contingent was able to convince the civilian concern that Stanley needed to be questioned before a determination of guilt, and the mob consented, stipulating that Stanley be taken to Temple instead of Belton. A 100-car, 300-man civilian "posse" escorted Stanley and his captors to Temple, its numbers increasing along the way.

While Stanley was in the process of being taken to the private office of Judge R. L. Cooper, the three Grimes children were buried together at the city cemetery and Mrs. Grimes's brother, Albert Nibling, stopped the lynching of an innocent African American man by cutting the rope that he was strung up by. The unidentified black suspect had worked for the Grimes family in the past and Nibling knew he was innocent. The mistaken suspect walked away from the lynching with severe rope marks around his neck.

Cooper's private office was in the Wilkerson Building, a three-story edifice in the business district of Temple. Officials apparently considered this location less conspicuous and therefore safer for the suspect. But they may also have favored its limited access; the sole entrance to the building was at the top of a narrow stairway.

In the end, their precautions were pointless. News of Stanley's arrival had spread swiftly through the community and in less than an hour a boisterous throng had gathered outside the building.

Stanley recounted his encounter and planned rendezvous with Harrison and Wells and Judge Cooper ordered their arrest and capture. Judge J. A. Humphries and two Temple police officers proceeded immediately to Rogers.

For the next few hours, the boisterous legion outside the Wilkerson Building thickened into a dangerous mob, reportedly chanting "Give us the Negro," intermittently engaging in "riotous" behavior and attempting to lay siege to the building's entrance. The *Temple Daily Telegram* would later downplay the mob's zeal, indicating that it was "not a mob, but a judicial body of good citizens determined that swift and terrible justice should be rendered once the guilty man was found."

After Harrison and Wells were arrested in Rogers, Temple officials reportedly requested and received a temporary "truce" with the mob, based on allowing Judge Humphries to deliver Harrison and Wells to Judge Cooper so their testimonies could be taken into account. Some reports say the agreed upon cessation in mob hostilities was set to last until 3 p.m. the following afternoon, but by evening the mob had dramatically supplemented its original numbers, reportedly swelling to 5,000-10,000 people. And after Harrison and Wells were delivered around 11 p.m., the multitude grew anxious.

When Harrison and Wells were questioned, discrepancies in their and Stanley's stories emerged and county officials kept press-

Front and back of a lynching postcard commemorating the "barbecue" of Will Stanley in Temple (Often mistakenly identified as Jesse Washington.). *Without Sanctuary: Lynching Photography in America.*

ing, cross-examining and re-examining, Harrison and Wells insisted Stanley had been the one in possession of the Grimes trousers instead of vice-versa, and that he had tried to trade them the trousers for a pair of shoes. Stanley was clearly the chief suspect, but some investigators and relatives of the victims insisted that the bloodbath perpetrated in the Grimes' residence would have made itself apparent on the guilty party's clothes, underclothes, etc. And, save his shirt, every article of Stanley's wardrobe was ripe with wear, even down to his sole-less shoes—but there wasn't a speck of blood on them.

The interrogations dragged on and just before midnight the mob decided it had had enough. Its bolder constituents stormed the Wilkerson Building's narrow stairwell entry, overran (or otherwise rendered ineffective) any law enforcement personnel who struck a defensive pose and seized Stanley. Harrison and Wells were immediately released because officials knew they had no way of protecting them. Both suspects ran for their lives.

The impatient mob marched Stanley down the shortest route to the public square in a procession the *Temple Daily Telegram* later described "as orderly as a circus parade." Once there, the throng (which now included women and children) pilfered nearby goods boxes and timber and built a fire. Just before the mob placed Stanley in the flames, an unidentified citizen confronted him, stating that Stanley knew himself to be guilty, but asking if anyone else was involved. According to the *Dallas Morning News*, Stanley's reply was thus:

> I know I am guilty as any of the rest, but I didn't do the killing. I held the horse while Slim Harris did the killing. We were hired to do it by a little low heavy-set white man who owns a dun horse and a good big buggy. Wait until tomorrow and I will take you to him and point him out, as I would know him anywhere.

The unidentified inquirer reportedly then kicked the fire away and asked the mob to wait, but another unidentified citizen shot Stanley and the crowd relegated him to the conflagration.

Stanley's body was dragged through the blaze repeatedly and, between the flames and the gunshot wound, he perished quickly, silenced after a few faint cries and moans. Later that morning, members of the mob retrieved Stanley's blackened torso (with charred, contorted and truncated limbs intact) and hung it from a large wooden post so photographs could be taken to commemorate the event (One of the images was used to create lynching postcards that were selling for ten cents apiece by August 5.).

On August 1, the *Temple Daily Telegram* coverage of the Stanley lynching took a strange turn. A page three headline said "Web Tightens Around White Man in the Grimes Murder." In the piece, the white man Stanley mentioned before his death is identified as the drug-addled husband of W. R. Grimes's sister, who wanted Mr. Grimes and the Grimes family to suffer because his estranged wife had conferred with her brother about divorcing him.

Sheriff Smith refused to comment on this possibility or the ongoing investigation that was being pursued in regards to it, but he did confirm that he thought that even if a white man had been involved, he still thought Stanley had done the killing. When questioned about the mob, Sheriff Smith was ill-disposed, but admitted that it was only Stanley they were after and refrained from condemnatory remarks:

> There was no one in that crowd who had any desire to hurt me, or anyone else but the nigger. I have no kick against anyone—I wanted to hold the negro a day or two for the information I hoped to get from him—I tried in every way to do this. I used every ruse and argument I could command to induce the crowd to let us keep him awhile. . . . We knew from the start we could never hope to get the negro out of town, therefore we did not intend to make the rash attempt. All that we hoped to do, and all we really tried to do was to defer the inevitable as long as possible in the hope of gaining more light on the deplorable Grimes tragedy, because we feared there were more people implicated, and that there is much in the bloody tragedy that has never been brought to light.

On August 2, Sheriff Smith said the "white man" theory had failed to develop and reiterated that he thought the Grimes murder was the work of one man, Will Stanley. On August 4, the "white man" theory was revisited in the *Daily Telegram* when Mr. Grimes's shaving razor was found wrapped in a cap at Rogers. On August 5, Bell County resident D. K. Northington and a group of like-minded skeptics of the lone black man theory found scraps of blood-stained underclothes in the remains of a recent campfire near a pool of water off the Santa Fe railroad tracks just southeast of the Grimes property. They also reportedly found an undershirt wrapped up and pinned to the bottom of the pool by a large rock.

1915

Law enforcement officials gave the recently discovered underclothes little credibility and, on August 8, the *Daily Telegram* published a story introducing and emphasizing Will Stanley's alleged past criminal record, presumably to bolster the theory of Stanley's guilt (or perhaps ease the community of Temple's collective conscience), suggesting that even if Stanley had been innocent or partially innocent in regards to the Grimes murders, he was surely guilty of other crimes.

On August 9, the *Daily Telegram* published editorials from other Texas communities that communicated their solidarity with the Temple lynch-mob. According to the *Brownwood News*, "the people of Temple need have no qualms of regret":

> They did wrong doubtless, but they did wrong very humanely. The fires of hell are a prophecy, but the fires of earth are a certainty, and they are put to a good service, we think, when they are employed to roast the cringing soul of a human vampire that beastly outrages women and wantonly murders little children.

The *Mart Herald* was mildly disapproving, but also empathetic:

> The burning of a negro murderer by a mob at Temple last week is another regrettable incident in the onward march of our civilization, yet it seems useless to sermonize. People will lose the power of self control under provocation when the test comes. Mobs are inexcusable, but they bring their lessons.

No members of the lynch-mob were ever prosecuted and the determination of Stanley's guilt was apparently never revisited. And though the "good county of Bell" enjoyed the endorsements of several communities around the state for the burning of Will Stanley, the event doesn't appear in George W. Tyler's 425-page *The History of Bell County* (The Naylor Company), published in 1936.

Mr. and Mrs. Grimes eventually recovered, W. R. living until September 2, 1952 and Annie making it until January 2, 1959.

One month later, on August 29, 1915, the second and third African American men were burned at the stake in Sulphur Springs, Texas.

Earlier on that day Hopkins County Sheriff J. B. Butler and Deputy Sheriff Nathan Asa Flippin traveled to a small community known as Tazewell (nine miles south of Sulphur Springs) and paid a visit to King and Joe Richmond, apparently intent on arresting

Now featuring a castle-themed playground, Buford Park was the site of two 1915 burnings at the stake in Sulphur Springs. *Author's collection.*

King for what some newspapers of the day referred to as a minor charge.[28] King reportedly resisted arrest and his brother Joe came to his defense. In the gun battle that ensued, Deputy Flippin was shot in the forehead and Sheriff Butler was shot in the head and arm. Flippin died instantly and Butler was disabled.

News of the killing spread rapidly and most of the adult male population of Hopkins County was searching for the Richmonds within hours. They tracked the brothers to a nearby wood and surrounded them. Then, according to a late, special August 29 edition of the *Sulphur Springs Gazette*, the Richmonds decided to give up. A Constable Smith and Hunt County Sheriff Akers told the Richmonds to put their hands in the air and "the negroes answered back, 'we surrender,' and put up their hands." What happened next was recorded in most newspapers of the day as a shoot-out. The hometown *Gazette* sets the record straight:

> Some one said one of the negroes only had one of his hands raised and has his pistol in the other. Some one shouted, "If you don't raise that other hand, we'll shoot; then some one, too eager or too nervous, fired, and the next instant the hills echoed with the report of twenty or twenty-five shots from pistols, shotguns, and rifles, both negroes fell and one of them was found dead, his head literally riddled with bullets while the other negro, though fatally injured was still living.

1915

The posse that captured King and Joe subsequently transported them to Sulphur Springs.

Hundreds of citizens were gathered at the square when the suspects arrived and the general consensus was that they should be burned at the stake. Sheriff Akers implored the growing mob to refrain from further malfeasance, but the crowd was unmoved. Sheriff Butler's wife repeated Sheriff Akers' request, but with the mob was resolute. One of Sheriff Butler's brothers made one last attempt to dissuade the mob, but, realizing its intractability, suggested that the deed should not be undertaken in the center of town. The lynch party debated the request and agreed to burn the Richmond brothers at Buford Park on the outskirts of town.

According to the *Gazette*, many members of the mob (and onlookers in general) had mistakenly assumed that both of the Richmonds were deceased. Joe was dead; King was simply unconscious. The burning was attended by 1,500-2,000 people and many were soon shocked to discover their mistake.

> Ready and willing hands supplied large lots of planks and 5 gallon cans of coal oil was poured over the funeral pier, a match was applied and the negroes were tossed into the flames. The flames revived the injured negro to where he raised up on his knees, twice, then fell back and gave up the ghost.

The August 29 *Gazette* reporting indicated that a law enforcement officer in Honey Grove had told Sulphur Springs officials that King had been wanted in Fannin County for shooting his wife and burning down his house with her body inside. The September 3 edition of the *Honey Grove Signal* indicated that King had reportedly attempted to murder his wife fifteen months earlier, but made no mention of her death or the firing of his home.

The burning of the Richmond brothers frightened a large number of the African American families in Sulphur Springs and the event resulted in a large black exodus from the community shortly thereafter.

Today, Sulphur Springs citizens still gather at Buford Park (at the corner of League Street and Connally Street), but for a different reason. The park is now home to a castle-themed playground, a public pavilion, gazebos, jogging trails, a basketball court and lighted baseball fields.

1916

> The strangest delusion in connection with lynching is that it is the victim who suffers most. In reality it is the community that is lynched. Waco did more than burn a Negro; she burned her own courage, decency and character, outraged the imaginations of her young people, and smeared a foul disgrace across her civic life.
>
> **San Francisco Bulletin**
> **circa 1916**

On Monday, May 15, 1916, an eighteen-year-old African American man named Jesse Washington was burned at the stake in Waco, Texas.

On May 8, a fifty-three-year-old white woman named Lucy Fryar was bludgeoned to death outside her home, seven miles south of the city. The chief and only suspect was Washington, an illiterate farm hand who worked for Lucy and her husband George.

Reported to have anger issues and mental disabilities, Washington allegedly left his cotton plow to get more seed from Mrs. Fryar. As she was measuring cotton seed out, she reportedly scolded him for his harsh treatment of the mules (attached to his plow) and Washington took offense, striking her in the head with a blacksmith's hammer. He then allegedly raped her and killed her with the hammer.

Afterwards, he supposedly resumed his work in the Fryar cotton field and then returned home to the cabin he shared with his parents. When the body of Mrs. Fryar was discovered, authorities immediately suspected Washington and found him whittling a stick in his parents' back yard.

McLennan County authorities arrested Washington and transported him to the county jail, but transferred him shortly thereafter.

1916

This photograph of a Waco mob watching the lynching of Jesse Washington was reportedly shot from the second floor office of Mayor John Dollins.
Courtesy of Library of Congress.

Considering the nature of the crime and the ethnicity of the chief suspect, they knew a lynching party would appear so they conveyed him to Dallas. On May 9, McLennan County Sheriff Sam S. Fleming and County Attorney John B. McNamara announced that Washington (who was still in Dallas County) had confessed (possibly under duress) and signed his "X" to a written confession. Sheriff Fleming and McNamara also reported that Washington had indicated where the murder weapon was located and officials reportedly discovered it in that very spot.

A McLennan County grand jury was subsequently convened and Washington was indicted in absentia. He was returned in the middle of the night on May 15, and stealthily delivered at 10 a.m. The courtroom his case was tried in had a capacity of 500 and was reportedly stuffed with 1,500 people. The trial, presided over by District Judge R. L. Munroe, began at 10 a.m. and was over before 11 a.m.

Washington pled guilty and before Judge Munroe had even finished recording the verdict, a large man in rear of the court room shouted "Get the Nigger." In seconds the mob was upon Washington, and Sheriff Fleming (who had ordered his men not to obstruct the

A photograph of the remains of Jessie Washington suspended from the tree used as the stake he was burned at. This image appeared in several newspapers across the country. *Courtesy of Library of Congress.*

anticipated vigilantism) and the court stenographer snuck out a side door while Judge Munroe watched helplessly (if not passively).

The mob secured Washington with a chain, dragged him out of the courthouse and then escorted him over to a yard next to Waco City Hall. While en route, he was "half-led, half-dragged and pushed all the time," members of the attending mob ripping off his clothes, slicing off one of his ears and several of his fingers, castrating him and stabbing him repeatedly (up to twenty-five times according to some accounts).

The mob had placed a large amount of kindling under a tree in the yard and when the grotesque procession reached it, the chain securing Washington (who was now covered in his own blood) was tossed over a sturdy limb. The conflagration was lit and Washington was hung by the chain over it. As the flames rose, the crowd (which now included women and children) roared with delight and Washington impossibly but reflexively attempted to climb the chain with his fingerless hands. As Washington was raised and lowered into the fire, Waco Mayor John Dollins watched from his 2nd floor city

1916

A photograph of Jesse Washington consigned to the smoldering coals. The photographer began selling lynching postcards of the event, but Waco citizens soon complained about the negative impressions the images created regarding the community. *Courtesy of Library of Congress.*

hall window and the Waco Chief of Police stood amongst the 10,000-15,000 person mob.

After the flames died down, Washington's charred torso (with flame-severed limbs) was raised high in the tree and the chain tied off so Waco citizens could get their picture taken with it. Then, pranksters on horseback cut Washington's remains down, placed the blackened cadaver in a tow sack and dragged it through the city streets. The torso was later attached to a car and drug to the Robinson community, where it was hung from a telephone pole.

A Waco photographer named Fred Gildersleeve chronicled the event and his pictures appeared in newspapers around the country. He would later immortalize some of the images in lynching postcards, but the citizens of Waco eventually grew squeamish and asked Gildersleeve to refrain from exploiting the incident. The photos were casting the entire community in a disturbing light.

1919

> There were in this case none of those unending delays which wear out jurors and inflame the patience of the public—features so regrettable in many of our criminal cases. Little evidence of the mob spirit was noticed until the negro's lawyers, having been refused a new trial, gave notice of an appeal. Then an infuriated public wracked its vengeance upon the black man.
>
> **Vernon Record**
> **January 24, 1919**

On January 20, 1919, an African American man named Bragg Williams was burned at the stake in Hillsboro, Texas.

On December 2, 1918, Annie Wells (wife of George) and her five-year-old son Curtis were beaten to death outside their home near Itasca. Their murderer utilized a blunt object to dispatch them and then carried their bodies into the house, setting it aflame to destroy any evidence. Neighbors saw smoke from the fire and retrieved the mother and son's remains before they were too badly burned.

Described by the *Waco News-Tribune* as "tall and ungainly, and seemingly of low mentality," Bragg Williams was captured less than three miles from the Wells residence. Before there had even been a full-throated accusation, a group of Hill County citizens attempted to lynch Williams, so he was transferred to Waco. Later, a group of Texas Rangers would transport him to Dallas and he would remain there until his trial date.

On January 16, Williams was escorted back to Hillsboro by the Texas Rangers and his trial began. Two well-regarded Hill County attorneys—Walter Collins and A. M. Frazier—were appointed to defend Williams and did so under protest. As attorneys for the prosecution and defense seated a jury, Williams sat in the courtroom under the constant guard of six Texas Rangers.

1919

A contemporary front page story on the Hillsboro lynching of Bragg Williams in an African American newspaper in Dallas. Note the poll tax payment reminder above the masthead. *Dallas Express*, 1919.

Collins and Frazier entered a "not guilty" plea for Williams, by reason of insanity. Williams was obviously mentally handicapped, but the prosecutors—well aware of Williams' "low mentality"—anticipated the defense team's plea and brought in Dr. W. L. Allison, a Fort Worth "alienist" (the contemporary term for a psychiatrist or psychologist in those days). Dr. Allison undermined the defense team's plea, insisting Williams was sane or at least not insane.

Williams never testified, but he did return to Hillsboro in the same yellow coveralls he had apparently left in, and the prosecution subsequently produced two white female witnesses who said they saw a black man in yellow coveralls heading in the direction of the Wells residence before the murder and a young black girl (named Smithy McDuffy) who claimed she saw a black man in yellow coveralls running from the direction of the residence after she had heard the screams of Annie Wells. Then, a white jailer named Jess Vanoy and Bragg's brother Natural were summoned and testified that Bragg had blood on his shoes the day he was captured. On Friday, January 17, Williams was convicted of murder and the Texas Rangers departed.

Ignoring the fact that it was obviously improbable that a man who was wearing yellow coveralls when he brutally beat a woman and her son to death with a blunt object would have noticeable blood on what were probably dark shoes and none on his light yellow coveralls, the case against Williams was strong; and that makes what happened after the guilty verdict curious.

On the morning of Monday, January 20, the court reconvened for sentencing and Judge Horton B. Porter condemned Williams to be hanged by the neck until dead on February 21. Collins and Frazier had defended Williams under protest and his guilty verdict was hardly an unpopular result; but once it was handed down and the death sentence imposed, Collins and Frazier surprisingly and unexpectedly requested a new trial. And when their petition for a retrial was denied, they filed a notice of appeal to the Court of Criminal Appeals.

At approximately 11:45 a.m., a mob—likely upset by the appeal and no longer in the mood for due process—assembled at the Hill County jail and demanded Williams be handed over. When the jailers refused, the mob stormed the facility and seized Williams from his cell. The lynch-mob dragged Williams to the courthouse square

1919

The Hillsboro corner (Elm and Covington) where Bragg Williams was dragged and burned at the stake after his defense team filed an appeal to his conviction (Hill County Courthouse in the background). *Author's collection.*

and tied him to a concrete "safety first" post at the corner of Elm Street and Covington Street.

Members of the mob quickly collected hay, wood and coal and piled them around Williams, dousing the combustibles in coal oil. A match was then applied and the blaze killed Williams in a matter of minutes. He put up no resistance, but was heard to exclaim "Help me, Cap" three times before the flames consumed him.

On January 21, Texas Governor William P. Hobby denounced the lynching and initiated steps to investigate it. On January 22, Governor Hobby sent a message to the Texas Legislature requesting legislation which would put an end to mob violence and correct the assumption that members of white lynch-mobs were not prosecutable. On January 23, Governor Hobby instructed Attorney General Calvin M. Cureton,[29] First Assistant Attorney General W. A. Keeling and E. A. Berry, Assistant Attorney General to the Court of Criminal Appeals, to begin investigations into Williams' lynching.

A Hill County grand jury subsequently examined charges against members of the lynch-mob and Judge Porter did his best to encourage impartiality. He sensed what the prosecution was up against and his instructions to the grand jury were specific and addressed the necessary integrity the jurors would have to uphold:

> The statute of this State provides your duty, provides the penalty for those who participate in a riot or in a mob or in a lynching. . . As your oath has prescribed, it is not a matter of friendship, of love or affection or of feeling. It is a matter prescribed by statute—my cold duty and your cold duty under the law.

Despite Judge Porter's charge, the grand jury adjourned without returning bills of indictment.

After a state investigation by First Attorney General Keeling, Attorney General Cureton and Assistant Attorney General Berry filed a motion to cite twelve members of the lynch-mob for contempt of court in regards to the Court of Criminal Appeals, because the vigilantes had lynched Williams after his appeal had been filed and was technically pending. In the absence of specific laws against lynching, it was a well-conceived attempt to prosecute members of the lynch-mob in a higher court, especially as it was obvious they wouldn't face prosecution in Hill County.

The motion was described as the first of its kind in Texas, but it, too, fell short. No action was taken on the motion in February or March and the effort eventually faded into obscurity.

1920

When one beholds how American citizens are being lynched, mobbed and burned at the stake in various parts of this country, while the authorities refuse to even attempt to apprehend the guilty culprits, it looks like democracy is a hollow mockery and the constitution of America and the laws of several states are mere scraps of paper.

                        Clifton F. Richardson, Sr.[30]
                        Houston Informer
                        July 10, 1920

On July 6, 1920 the third and fourth African American men were burned at the stake in the Paris, Texas area.

After fighting for his country in World War I, a twenty-eight-year-old African American man named Herman Arthur returned home having glimpsed a world far removed from the Jim Crow South. He joined his parents, Scott and Violet Arthur (both of whom had been born into slavery) in Paris and began working as a sharecropper for sixty-one-year-old J. H. Hodges and his thirty-four-year-old son, William. Herman lived in a sharecropper shack with his parents, his eighteen-year-old brother Ervin, three sisters (aged fourteen, seventeen and twenty) and his six-year-old nephew, Ervin Hill (named after his eighteen-year-old uncle).

The sharecropper arrangement the Arthurs had with the Hodges was a losing proposition and it eventually grew worse. The Hodges demanded that they work six days a week instead of five, and when the Arthurs skipped a Saturday on May 26, J. H. and William appeared at their shack unannounced (on Thursday, July 1), looking to have a word with Herman. When they discovered only two of the Arthur girls at the shack, they threw out the food the girls had been cooking and kicked the family's stove into the yard. Then they made the two sisters undress, confiscating their clothing because they considered the Arthur family in arrears for not working the previous Saturday. When the rest of the family returned, they realized the situation was no longer tenable.

On July 2 the Arthurs began packing their things, but the Hodges reappeared with their guns up; Herman and Ervin responded in kind. According to a letter to the *New York Age*, J. H. and William fired on the Arthurs first and when Herman and Ervin fired back, J. H. was shot in the head and William was shot in the neck. Both men succumbed to their wounds and Herman and Ervin fled.

A massive manhunt was conducted, but the Arthur brothers had already escaped to Oklahoma. In their absence, an enraged number of the white population seized the rest of the Arthur family and placed them in the Lamar County jail "for their own protection."

There are different versions of what happened next.

In 1980, a sixty-six-year-old Ervin Hill told the *Chicago Tribune* that Herman and Ervin returned to Paris of their own volition because they had heard the rest of their family was going to be lynched in their stead. In 1998, a ninety-one-year-old retired, white civil attorney and Paris resident named Hardy Goodner Moore told the *Tribune* that the Arthur brothers were captured near Valiant, Oklahoma after they were betrayed by a black resident named Pitt McGrew.[31] Whatever the case, Herman and Ervin returned to Paris and were placed in the county jail alongside the rest of their family.

The Arthur brothers told their story and claimed self–defense, but the facts in the case were irrelevant. Several unruly factions of the white citizenry were not amicable to a trial and signs that announced Herman and Ervin's lynching began appearing around town. Lamar County Judge Ben H. Denton attempted to dissuade the effort, assuring his constituents that the suspects would have a speedy trial, but they didn't want to wait.

At 7:30 p.m. on July 6, the Arthur brothers were removed from the county jail and taken to the Lamar County fairgrounds (on the northern edge of Paris). A lynch-mob chained them to a flagpole, tortured them and then burned them to a crisp as a crowd of 3,000 citizens looked on. Their smoldering remains were then dragged via automobile through the African American section of the city, their executioners all the while screaming "Here are the barbecued Niggers."

Scott and Violet Arthur and their grandson Ervin Hill were subsequently released, but the Arthur sisters remained in custody. They were reportedly beaten and raped repeatedly by twenty white men and then given a bucket of molasses, a sack of flour and some bacon and advised to make themselves scarce.

The Arthur sisters eventually rejoined their father, mother and nephew and hid in the local woods until members of a local African American Masonic Lodge and a handful of white neighbors helped them escape.

On July 7, the *Paris News* reported that factions of the black community in Paris "were assembling and would seek revenge" for the Arthur brothers' lynching that night. That evening dozens of white citizens looted guns and ammunition from local hardware stores and stood at the ready in the town square. The black "uprising" never materialized and Paris Mayor J. Morgan Crook spent the following day traveling from crowd to crowd attempting to diffuse white paranoia.

The bodies of Herman and Ervin were recovered separately and a day apart. According to the *Paris News* they were buried at an undisclosed location in Lamar County. According to the *Chicago Tribune*, they were buried in the town's earliest African American cemetery a short distance from the fairgrounds. The *Tribune* also noted that a middle-class subdivision for blacks was later built on top of the cemetery.

Several elements inside and outside the state of Texas believed that the Arthurs had been innocent because they acted in self-defense, and some officials suggested they were innocent altogether because they hadn't been involved in the shooting at all. According to the *New York Times*, Lamar County Sheriff William Everett "Eb" Clarkson told McCurtain County (Oklahoma) Sheriff U. W. Dewitt he was sure that one if not both of the lynched Arthur brothers was innocent.

On July 9, the National Association for the Advancement of Colored People protested the act of lawlessness and on July 10 a special Lamar County grand jury convened to inquire into the lynching. Nothing came out of the protest or the grand jury investigation and hundreds of African Americans consequently left Paris.

What was left of the Arthur family arrived in Chicago on August 30, 1920. A prominent black doctor named W. W. Lucas met them at the train station and took them to the Chicago Urban League to set up temporary housing. The influential African American newspaper the *Chicago Defender* organized a fund for the Arthurs and eventually raised enough money for them to get their own home. Chicagoans embraced the Arthurs and they began a new life. Scott Arthur died in 1937 at the age of 101. Violet passed in 1951 at the age of ninety-seven.

Hill characterized Violet as more a mother to him than a grandmother and, though he marveled at her strength over the years, he knew she never completely got over the lynching. "There were times long after we all grew up that she would go into a room by herself," he said, "and just moan and groan about Uncle Ervin, her baby boy, and Uncle Herman."

After Herman and Ervin Arthur were burned at the stake in Paris, Texas, the rest of the family fled north, arriving in Chicago on August 30, 1920. Scott and Violet Arthur are the third and fifth persons from the left and their grandson Ervin is the little boy front and center. The lynched brothers' sisters stand on either side of little Ervin and farthest right in the back. *Courtesy of the Chicago History Museum.*

1920

In Autumn of 1920, an unidentified African American man was reportedly burned to death near Terrell, Texas, but the incident only came to light because of a fissure in the Ku Klux Klan years later.

In 1927, five former Klansmen decided to break away from the main body of the "Invisible Empire" and carry on as a separate entity. Dr. H. W. Evans, the presiding Imperial Wizard of the KKK, filed an injunction suit against them and initially requested $100,000 in compensation for damages (later increased to $500,000), planning to make an example of the offshoot.

The Ku Klux Klan boasted a membership of approximately 2,000,000 American citizens (almost 1.7% of the U. S. population at the time) and had gotten governors elected in twelve states. With friends in high places, Evans was confident the Klan would emerge victorious; but the litigation played out in a Federal Court in Pittsburgh, Pennsylvania and the defendants made the most of the public forum.

Defense witnesses exposed Klan secrets and testified to multiple incidents of Klan violence, terrorism and murder. The most shocking account involved an African American man in the Terrell area.

According to the testimony of former Dallas Klan member named Clarence W. Ludlow, "the fate of a colored man had been debated in the Dallas lodge" and members later "tarred and oiled" the man and set him on fire. Evans denied the allegation (and the rest of the charges), but Federal Judge W. H. S. Thompson upheld the testimony offered by the defendants and dismissed the KKK's suit. The court's opinion was plain and pointed:

> In the state of Texas men were brought before the Klan, tried and convicted, and in some instances were subjected to brutal beatings, and in others were condemned to death and burned at the stake. . . This unlawful organization, so destructive to the rights and liberties of the people, has come in vain asking this court of equity for injunctive or other relief. They come with filthy hands and can get no assistance here.[32]

The KKK's Terrell victim was never identified and no charges were ever brought against Klan members in his lynching.

1921

> The mob that burned the negro lynched the law and temporarily overrode constitutional government in Camp County, without excuse, even if not without provocation. They permitted the mob spirit to manifest itself in a particularly atrocious form, and the State adds another to the long list of disgraces of this sort to its record. Texas moves up a notch in the contest among the States for the dishonor of making a record in mob murders.
>
> *Houston Post*
> **October 14, 1921**

On August 15, 1921, the body of an African American man named Alex Winn was burned in Coolidge, Texas.

According to the *Breckenridge Daily American*, Winn was accused of assaulting a seven-year-old white girl in Datura; according to the *Dallas Morning News*, he was accused of assaulting a white woman. Whoever his alleged victim was, Winn was immediately hanged by an angry mob in Datura, and then deposited at an undertaking establishment in Coolidge.

A second mob removed Winn's body from the undertaker's office, doused it in kerosene and burned it to a crisp in a Coolidge street.

On October 10, 1921, a nineteen-year-old African American man named Wylie McNeely was burned at the stake in Leesburg, Texas.

On October 9, an eight-year-old white girl named Irene King was allegedly attacked while walking home from Sunday school. In her own words, she passed a patch of trees (about a half-mile from her father's farm) and she experienced something like a coat being thrown over her head and lost consciousness. What exactly happened after that was never made clear, but Camp County Sheriff John J. Reese concluded that King spent approximately one hour in the woods and, regardless of what occurred, the suspect was Mc-

A banner headline in a McKinney newspaper announced the lynching of Wylie McNeely. *Weekly Democrat-Gazette*, 1921.

Neely. There was no mention or suggestion that King was physically or sexually assaulted, and, though McNeely was the only suspect, he was discovered sitting in front of a store in Leesburg, the crime seemingly unbeknownst to him.

Sheriff Reese transported McNeely to the Camp County seat of Pittsburg (seven miles east) and he was charged with assault with the intent to rape and assault with the attempt to murder. Fearing local reprisals, Sheriff Reese took McNeely to the Mount Pleasant jail in Titus County (twelve miles to the north). A small mob appeared outside the jail that evening, but (according to the *Plano Star-Courier*) a "lack of leadership" hindered their intentions.

On October 10, Sheriff Reese learned that hundreds of Leesburg vigilantes were en route to Mount Pleasant in a 100-car procession. As sunset approached, Reese and Titus County law enforcement officials decided to transfer McNeely, instructing him to climb out the back window of the Mount Pleasant jail instead of leaving out the front door. A car was waiting, but elements of a lynch-mob had already taken up positions around the jail and snatched McNeely as he came out the window. The Leesburg contingent joined McNeely's captors and the entire mob headed back to the location of the alleged crime.

The growing horde (now comprised of citizens of Camp, Titus and other counties) arrived back in Leesburg at 9 p.m., and McNeely was taken to a vacant lot on the outskirts of town. Members of the mob drug a large tree stump into the middle of a street and affixed an upright steel rail to it. McNeely was suspended from the top of the rail and the mob piled lumber and brush up to a point just below his feet and saturated the timber in coal oil.

McNeely confessed, but to what is unknown—probably to whatever his tormentors wanted him to.

In fact, the *Port Arthur News* reported that McNeely's exact words were" "I did it. I did it. I won't ne'er do it again." McNeely was apparently pleading with his executioners in hopes of a reprieve, possibly not even aware of what he was confessing to. Then:

> A match flared. A burst of flame. A few terrible shrieks and the black form was still as the fire burned high. It remained there throughout the night.

The next morning all that was left of McNeely was a few bones protruding from a drift of ash.

1922

> Lynching of blacks, even burning, was as common in the United States in 1922 as changes in the weather. Other countries and other peoples devised their own quirky methods of doing away with their citizens, but in America, the atrocity of choice was lynching, and its heyday was from the end of the Civil War to 1923.
>
> **Monte Akers**
> *Flames After Midnight: Murder, Vengeance and the Desolation of a Texas Community* **(1999)**

On May 4, 1922, a seventeen-year-old, white schoolgirl named Eula Ausley was brutally murdered about two-and-a-half miles outside of Kirven. Ausley had stayed late at school to practice a play with her classmates and was on her way home when she was attacked.

As her horse was found tied off to a fence not far from where she died, it's possible she knew her assailant(s) and had stopped to visit with him (or them) and may even have been helped off her horse. Nearby farmers later admitted to hearing her screams, but hadn't felt compelled to investigate them at the time.

Her lifeless body was discovered at approximately 9 p.m.; her head had been bashed in and mashed to a pulp. The *Waco-Times Herald* reported that "her throat had been cut, her head was crushed and there were about twenty-seven stab wounds in her face and the upper portion of her body. Other accounts indicated that Ausley was found nude and her tongue had been cut out.

Freestone County sheriff Horace Mayo had no clues and no promising suspects. A few days into the investigation it was learned that a local African American field hand named Snap Curry had arrived home with blood on his shirt sleeves on the evening of Ausley's murder and, even though he had participated in the search for the girl's killers, he immediately became the chief suspect. When Curry became aware of the white community's suspicions, he fled and was captured.

On the evening of May 5, Curry's captors coerced a confession out of him. Curry's testimony allegedly implicated two other African Americans, Mose Jones and Johnnie Cornish. Mose Jones was a forty-six-year-old, long-time resident of Kirven. He was the father of three and had actually named one of his children after the town and another after Otis King, a successful, local, white farmer that he worked for part-time. Johnnie Cornish was the nineteen-year-old illegitimate son of a respected, though recently deceased local white man. He had just gotten married a few weeks earlier.

After Curry's confession, Jones and Cornish were arrested and joined Curry in the Freestone County jail in Fairview. Later that evening, vigilantes removed Curry, Jones and Cornish from the jail and transported them back to Kirven in a 165-car motorcade.

It was after midnight when the lynching party reached Kirven, but most of the town came out to take part in the spectacle. The mob chose a vacant field between the Methodist and Baptist churches to stage its vengeance and gathered wood from a stack available at a nearby drugstore. The makeshift stake was a heavy, iron "sulky" riding plow that was either delivered to the lot for the occasion or already sitting there. The vigilantes affixed Curry to the seat of the plow and stacked up kindling around him. They then castrated him, poured gasoline over the timber and applied a match. As the flames leapt up around him, Curry began singing an old church hymn called "O Lord I am Coming."

Curry expired in a matter of minutes and when the flames severed his bonds, he fell over face first into the fire. As the smell of burning flesh fouled the night air, Jones and Cornish vociferously denied involvement in Ausley's gruesome murder, but to no avail.

The plow was too hot to tie Jones to so the mob simply bound him with a long rope and started to pull him back and forth, into and out of the blaze. After the first circuit, Jones attempted to run and his child's namesake, Otis King, struck him in the face with a radius rod from a Model T Ford; the blow knocked one of Jones' eyeballs loose. Stunned and disoriented, Jones tried to wipe his face and the eyeball and connective tissue stuck to the back of his hand. Before he could make sense of what he saw with his remaining eye,

A banner headline in a Brownwood newspaper reported a multiple burning at the stake in Kirven, but the "stake" was actually a sulky riding plow.
Brownwood Bulletin, 1922.

the mob jerked him back into the flames and immobilized him there. He was dead in six minutes.

Even in the face of certain annihilation, Cornish was defiant. After the mob tied him up and subjected him to one circuit into and out of the conflagration, he reversed course and dove into the flames headfirst, clutching the red-hot plow blade. He then thrust his face into the heart of the blaze and inhaled deeply, hastening his demise and robbing the sadistic vigilantes of a prolonged torment.

Members of the mob stacked all three corpses together and piled on more wood. The remains of the suspects were cremated by the time daylight broke.

The May 6 edition of the *Houston Chronicle* would later report that "the blackest entry in Texas' history of crime had been chalked down on the records against the negro trio—and the general feeling was that the mob of 600 did a 'good job' in the early hours of the

A 1920 advertisement for a Sulky riding plow like the one used in the lynching of Snap Curry, Mose Jones and Johnnie Cornish. The actual plow remained at the site of the atrocity for years, a stark reminder to black citizens in the area. *Abilene Reporter*, 1897.

1922

Photograph of the field that Snap Curry, Mose Jones and Johnnie Cornish were burned in. *Author's collection.*

morning."

After the incineration of Curry, Jones and Cornish, the perpetrating white community indulged in farcical rumors that suggested that the local African American population was planning a "rising," and this fabrication roused whites to lynch several more blacks in the region, but no more by fire. The resultant homicidal rampage (licensed by white paranoia) lasted a month, leaving innocent, black men dead all over Freestone County, hanging in trees, lying bullet-riddled in fields and hastily disposed of in shallow graves.

Eventually, a white doctor from Fairview came forward and demonstrated Cornish's innocence. In time, Jones was exonerated as well. According to Monte Akers' authoritative book on the Kirven lynching, *Flames After Midnight: Murder, Vengeance, and the Desolation of a Texas Community* (1999), Curry may have been an unwitting accomplice, but two local white men—Claude and Audrey Powell—actually murdered Eula Ausley.

Two weeks later, after a trio of innocent African American men were burned in Kirven, an apparently guilty one became the second black man burned at the stake in Texarkana.

Early on May 19, an African American man named Huley Owen

was arrested for stealing "automobile casings and other appliances." In jail, Owen told Texarkana police officers he would take them to where a stolen battery was hidden, so they transferred him to a police car and headed for the spot. Upon arrival, Officer Dick Choate and Chief of Police A. J. Lummus allowed Owen to step ahead and uncover the stolen goods; but instead of revealing the stolen items, Owen reportedly retrieved a firearm and shot Choate. Chief Lummus responded by shooting Owen in the face, but the shot went through his cheek and Owen fled to a nearby car and drove away. Miller County (located on the Arkansas side of Texarkana) Sheriff John Strange fell in behind Owen in a police car and followed him to the outskirts of town, whereby Owen abandoned the vehicle and fled to a small pond where he reportedly attempted to drown himself. Sheriff Strange pulled Owen out of the pond and transported him to a local hospital. Officer Choate was taken to a different hospital and died on an operating table.

Owen was eventually transferred to the Miller County jail, but he didn't remain there long. Just after 8 p.m., a mob broke down the jail door with a makeshift battering ram and seized him. The vigilantes transported Owen to Offenhauser Park and shot him to death. They then dragged his body to the corner of Front Street and Vine Street (one block east of the Texas/Arkansas state line), covered it with kindling, doused it with kerosene and burned it to a crisp.

On Saturday, June 10, eight white men were arrested in the lynching of Huley Owen and, on June 12, Circuit Court Judge George R. Haynie set their bails at $5,000 each. In the coming months the white defendants' trials were repeatedly postponed and rescheduled and none were ever convicted.

On the same day Huley Owen was burned in Texarkana, a nineteen-year-old African American man named Joe Winters was accused of assaulting a fourteen-year-old white girl near Leonidas (five miles west of Conroe). He immediately fled and was tracked down by bloodhounds on the afternoon of May 20.

Winters' captors delivered him to the alleged victim's home and she positively identified him. After Winters' identity was confirmed, he was transported to Conroe.

In Conroe, Winters' escort transmogrified into a mob of at least

1922

THE LOOKING GLASS

THE BURNING BODY

the world needs your giftless as a Battle Axe of Cleavage, more as a Power for welding. I have lived in Baltimore 15 years and by fact of official connection have served on committees with New Yorkers and Bostonians and may be said, I believe, to know my neighbors both North and South, and it is no truer than "Pigs is Pigs" than that "Folks is Folks," and Hate begets Hate and 'tis a seed with a great yield. Now, why so hard? Why so intolerant?

ALLIE M. COPELAND,
Baltimore, Md.

* * *

We turn to our other mail. There are two pictures, a clipping and three letters. Here are the pictures and the clipping from a Texas paper, the name of which was not sent:

The burning of Joe Winters in the public square at Conroe, Texas, drew a larger crowd than the annual visit of the circus. Winters was accused of attacking a 14-year-old white girl. Bloodhounds were used to capture him and he was chased through three counties. Newspapers advertised the event and thousands of persons, including young women and children, watched him chained to a peg in the public square and a match applied to his clothing saturated with gasoline.

* * *

Then comes a letter from Florida:

It might be interesting to know that on the night of the 14th of July, Jake Davis, of Colquit, Ga., was lynched, charged with being the father of a child by a white woman. It appears that the woman gave birth to a Negro child and her neighbors insisted that she tell the father of the child, which she did with the usual result. The interesting fact is that the State press took no notice of it. It was not in the papers.

* * *

Then a white man writes from Denton, Texas:

Have you a few moments of leisure to give your attention to the following? Recently the white population of this little town came to the conclusion that a park is needed. Their eyes fell upon one of the Negro sections through which a creek lined with trees flows. This section was considered undesirable, but good enough for Negroes: there they lived for years, built humble homes, now they have to

"A LARGER CROWD THAN . . . THE CIRCUS"

This page featuring images from the Conroe lynching of Joe Winters appeared in the November 1922 edition of the N.A.A.C.P.'s *Crisis* magazine.

1,000 citizens (including women and children). When the boisterous throng secured him to a stake at the northeast corner of the courthouse square, he allegedly confessed while members of the mob gathered kindling and piled it around him. They saturated the kindling and Winters' clothes in coal oil and then applied a match. Winters was dead in a matter of minutes.

In later years the narrative used to lynch Winters was set straight.

Like Ted Smith and Viola Delancey, Winters and the unidentified white girl had apparently been romantically involved and carried on in private; when a white man caught them together in the woods, the girl blamed Winters and claimed he had forced himself on her. Winters was obviously dispatched before this version of the affair was acknowledged.

On May 26, 1922, a second African American man was burned in Waco, Texas

At approximately 9 p.m. on May 25, while out driving four miles north of Waco on Corsicana Road, Harold Bolton and Maggie Hays (both white), were reportedly accosted by a large African American male. According to Hays, as Bolton attempted to turn his car around, the assailant walked up to the driver-side door with a gun and shot Bolton four times, killing him instantly. The assailant then grabbed Hays and took her into the woods, allegedly raping her.

Three hours later, as a Katy freight train (headed to Fort Worth) approached, the assailant reportedly attempted to shoot Hays, but his weapon jammed. He pushed her down instead and departed to jump the train.

Hays later ran into three white men who phoned McLennan County Deputy Sheriff Marvin "Red" Burton at 1 a.m. A car was sent to transport Hays to Waco and Deputy Burton met her at the city limits. Deputy Burton questioned her as they proceeded to her residence in East Waco, where she lived with her father, Sam Harris.

After hearing Hays' account of the incident, the McLennan County Sheriff's Department sent officers up Corsicana Road and contacted authorities along the Katy run to Fort Worth and instructed them to keep an eye out for the suspect. Of her assault, Hays said "He took me off into the woods and treated me awful... he treated me so brutally. I don't know how I can live through it." Of her assailant, Hays said "He was a big negro and had a very prominent gold tooth. I was with him so long that I know every feature of his face."

Later in the day, an African American man named Sank Johnson was brought by the Harris residence by the Waco police for identification. Hays indicated that Johnson was the wrong man. Then, just after 5 p.m., one of Harris' neighbors, E. L. McClure, dragged Jesse Thomas, a twenty-three-year-old African American service car driver with a gold tooth into the Harris living room.

Recently deputized, McClure had spotted Thomas downtown, a gold tooth presumably the only clue making him a suspect. McClure had then asked Thomas to cut his grass, but, instead of taking Thomas to his house, delivered him to Harris', where McClure and two other men seized him and took him inside. When Harris asked Hays if Thomas was her assailant, she said "That's the man, papa," and Harris drew an automatic pistol he had concealed in his clothes and began shooting. Thomas broke free and fled, but Harris hit him with seven shots. Thomas collapsed dead in the front yard and Harris drug his body to a side street.

When a passerby queried Harris about the dead body, he replied "Just say that Sam Harris killed that nigger."

The remains of Jesse Thomas were subsequently conveyed to a local undertaker, but only briefly. In less than an hour, a mob of hundreds apparently stormed the undertaker's establishment and retrieved Thomas' body. They then tied it to a car and drug it through the city en route to the city plaza.

At the plaza, they built a fire and then tossed Thomas' body into it. Thousands of Waco citizens watched Thomas burn and then members of the mob re-tied his charred corpse to a car and drug it back through the city (and past the Harris residence).

Meanwhile, the family of Jesse Thomas presented compelling evidence that he had been home on Thursday, May 25, and could not have murdered Bolton or assaulted Hays. And Waco Chief of Police, Lee Jenkins, concurred, indicating that he thought Sank Johnson (who was still in custody) was the culprit.

When word spread that Harris may have killed an innocent man, he presented himself at the office of a local constable and offered to surrender. No complaint had been filed against him so he was released.

On January 29, 1923, an African American man named Roy

Mitchell was arrested in connection with a slew of murders. He was indicted for and eventually convicted of six homicides, including that of Harold Bolton (whose watch authorities found in Mitchell's possession during their investigation). Mitchell confessed to Bolton's murder but later maintained that his confession was coerced. In the subsequent trials regarding these charges, juries involved in his convictions sometimes spent less than five minutes on their decisions.

On February 13, 1923, the *Brownwood Bulletin* suggested that—the short deliberations notwithstanding—the fact that Mitchell was even afforded trials was progress and alluded to the Thomas lynching:

> It is probably because of a lynching there last year that there has been no mob action in the case of the negro Mitchell, now held under charges of having slain five white persons and having assaulted three white women. For one of the crimes which Mitchell has admitted is the same crime for which a negro was unlawfully killed last year after having been identified by his victim; and that negro's body was burned in the center of the city while thousands of vengeance-mad Waco citizens danced in glee around the fire. The mob has learned that it can be mistaken; that the justice it administers is sometimes not justice, but murder.

On July 30, 1923, Roy Mitchell was hanged until dead at the McLennan County jail. For decades he would be listed as the last man legally hanged in Texas, but research suggests that unfortunate distinction actually belonged to Nathan Lee, executed at the Brazoria County Courthouse in Angleton on August 31, 1923. Lee, forty-years-old at the time of his execution, was also African American.

There is no mention of Maggie Hays ever being called to identify or testify against Mitchell. There is also no mention of a complaint in the murder of Jesse Thomas ever being filed against Sam Harris.

On December 11, 1922, a twenty-year-old, white school teacher named Florine Grayson was reportedly attacked by an African American man outside her home in Streetman, Texas (eight miles north of Kirven) at approximately 6:45 a.m. Her assailant allegedly threw a sack over her head and attempted to "choke her into insensibility," but Grayson apparently "frustrated the negro's designs" and made it back to her porch, where she fainted.

News of the attack spread rapidly and people poured into Streetman to assist in apprehending the culprit. A twenty-five-year-old African American man named George Gay was picked up three hours later and approximately three miles outside of town after a hat presumed to be his was spotted not far from the scene of the assault. Then, according to the *Dallas Morning News*:

> A well-known resident here at 11:15 a.m. delivered an impassioned plea to hundreds of citizens from Freestone, Limestone and Navarro Counties, asking them not to harm the suspect until bloodhounds from the Ferguson State Farm arrived to assist in identification. He said that he was a lifelong friend of the family, and made this request on behalf of the widowed mother of the girl. The crowd heard the plea in silence.
>
> Convinced by the temper of the crowd that the negro would either be hanged or burned, as wood had already been stacked in the street, County Attorney J. E. Woods and Sheriff Mayo attempted to carry Gay to the Fairfield jail.

Woods and Sheriff Mayo—who had seen Snap Curry, Mose Jones and Johnnie Cornish snatched from the Fairfield jail and burned at the stake just six months earlier—were stopped by a mob on Teague Road and relieved of their suspect. Gay was spared the torch, but white vigilantes strung him up in a tree with chains and riddled his body with 300 bullets. The tri-county mob's pyromania was apparently satisfied later when the only African American hotel in Streetman was burned to the ground.

Later accounts undermined Grayson's version of the assault. Some indicated that Grayson had surprised an African American in her outhouse and simply fainted as he fled. Others suggested she had been caught with a black man rather than being assaulted by one.

Grayson was treated for a few scratches and recovered quickly. Gay's guilt was never officially established and Mayo eventually recovered his remains.

1924

The negro in the South who is worthy, industrious, and who manifests a desire to live peacefully with his white neighbors never lacks for assistance from white friends in improving his lot. In the South there is not that prejudice against seeing the negro get ahead economically that is found in the North. As for the "Jim Crow" canard, the negro who objects to that usually hails from the North, where the uplifters fail to distinguish between the terms segregation and discrimination.

Houston Post
July 18, 1924

On July 23, 1924, a nineteen-year-old African American man named Jesse Davis was burned at the stake in southern Victoria County.

Davis was a convict working at a county road camp near Dernal (just west of Farm Road 404 between Victoria and Bloomington). The bunkhouse that Davis and three other African Americans prisoners were confined to was infested with bugs. They reportedly sprayed their bunks with gasoline "to kill vermin" and an overheated lantern apparently ignited their bedding. As the prisoners awoke and fled, Davis was the first one to the door but his right leg was chained to a bedpost and he could not exit the structure. Davis perished in the inferno and his three bunk mates were severely burned.

Why Davis was the sole African American prisoner chained to his bedpost in the bunk house is never made clear. The limited information on his death doesn't imply that he was maliciously singled out for chaining or that the structure itself was torched on purpose. But in a period when the domiciles of many African Americans in Texas were little more than "huts" (and were openly referred to as such), the structure housing Davis and his bunkmates probably mimicked conditions outside the work camp. The African

1924

American quarters were probably less sufficient for habitation than that of their white counterparts and Davis' death (and his bunk mates' injuries) could surely be attributed to the conditions they endured as less-entitled citizens of the state.

1930

Sherman is the chief sufferer; it is the city and the people of the city who are the chief victims of the mob. Not alone will they have suffered almost unprecedented property damage, but they also must stand for a time under a flood of condemnation which will pour in upon them from all over the country.

> *Fort Worth Star-Telegram*
> **May 11, 1930**

On May 9, 1930, a forty-one-year-old African American man named George Hughes was asphyxiated and then burned to a crisp in Sherman, Texas.

Hughes had moved to the area from Honey Grove a few months before and labored on various farms before going to work for Ned Farlow approximately five miles south of Sherman. According to reports, Hughes had grown frustrated with Farlow over back pay by late April.

At 10 a.m. on Saturday, May 3, Hughes reportedly stopped working the fields and headed to the Farlow residence carrying a double-barreled shotgun. A neighbor called the Grayson County Sheriff's Department (from a nearby cotton gin) and Deputy Sheriff Bart Shipp responded. By the time Deputy Shipp arrived, Hughes had left the Farlow home and was walking into an alfalfa field. When Hughes spotted Deputy Shipp's vehicle, he fired on it twice, one shot going through the windshield. Deputy Shipp emerged from his vehicle uninjured and, as Hughes' shotgun was emptied, arrested him.

It is unclear what transpired at the Farlow residence, but it can be assumed that Mrs. Farlow was alone and Hughes made an ill-advised visit to address unresolved issues of unpaid wages. Whatever

1930

A Sherman mob outside the Grayson County Courthouse watches as one of their own attempts to start a fire on the first floor. Governor Dan Moody eventually placed the entire Sherman community under martial law for two weeks. *Fort Worth Star-Telegram*, 1930.

occurred, Hughes was later charged with criminal assault. One account suggested Hughes had bound Mrs. Farlow's hands and feet with bailing wire; another report stated that Hughes had sexually assaulted Mrs. Farlow.

Due to the volatile nature of the charges, Grayson County authorities had Hughes transferred out of the county jail for his own safety. On Tuesday, May 6, a white mob attempted to seize Hughes and law enforcement personnel confronted the vigilantes, firing into the air to warn them off. District Attorney Joe Cox appeared and informed the mob that Hughes was not in the facility, but the mob was distrustful and requested that Cox allow a mob "committee" to search the jail. Cox permitted the search and the committee was unable to find Hughes.

After the mob's first attempt to grab Hughes, Grayson County authorities contacted state officials and requested assistance from the Texas Rangers. On May 7, Texas Ranger Captain Frank Hamer,[33] Sgt. J. B. Wheatley, J. E. McCoy and J. W. Aldrich left Austin at 4:25 p.m.

and arrived in Sherman that evening.

On March 9, Hughes' short-lived trial began and the events that followed are best conveyed by eye-witness participant, Captain Hamer:

> On the morning of the 9th of May the negro was brought into the court room. The jury was empaneled, the trial proceeded to get under way. It was while the first State witness was on the stand testifying, that the crowd made a rush on the District Court room to get the prisoner and in their attempt to do so, two double doors opening into a hallway near the District Court room were broken down. The District Judge [R. M. Carter] ordered the prisoner locked up in the District Attorney's [second-story] vault and then we immediately proceeded to disperse the mob, which we did by use of our guns, without firing, and tear gas bombs. The District Judge and other officials then decided that a change of venue should be ordered in the case. The crowd made two other attempts to rush the court room on the second floor and was beaten back each time.
>
> I instructed my men that the next time they rushed the courthouse that I would fire on the mob, but for them to hold their fire until I gave orders to shoot. In a few minutes the mob attempted to rush the court room again, coming up the stairways and I fired a shotgun loaded with buckshot, wounding two men, so it was reported to us, this stopped the mob. I had heard a number of them say prior to the time that I fired on them, that "you can't shoot us." It never occurred to me what they meant until a newspaper man came up stairs and showed me a message that he said he had received over the A. P. wires reading as from the Governor, "protect the negro if possible, but do not shoot anybody". I informed him that I had received no such message, however, at this time, this report seemed to have been well-circulated among the crowd.
>
> I saw the District Judge and told him about this report and informed him that I didn't believe the Governor would issue such orders, because we probably could not hold the prisoner if such order was issued. One of the agitators walked to the foot of the stairway and asked me if I was going to give the prisoner up to them, I told him we were not, he says "well we are coming up to get him", I said "any time you feel lucky, come on, but when you start up the stairway once more, there is going to be many funerals in Sherman". For twenty or thirty minutes, things were quiet.

1930

> They started breaking windows down stairs, the sheriff and deputies had previously gone down stairs, leaving myself and men to guard the negro and the stairways, then all at once the flames from the lower story of the courthouse swept up the stairways and on up to the ceiling over our heads to the second floor and myself and men barely escaped the burning building. The flames cut us off from the vault and we could not have opened the vault if we could have gotten to it, as we did not know the combination, so we came out and down into the crowd.

When the mob was unsuccessful at taking custody of Hughes by force and then couldn't get Captain Hamer to relinquish custody of him, vigilantes threw gasoline into the basement (or somewhere along the first floor) and ignited it. As squadrons of the Sherman Fire Department arrived and attempted to fight the blaze, members of the mob held them back and severed their fire hoses.

When 300 National Guardsmen (sent by Governor Moody) arrived to assist the Rangers in getting the situation under control, the mob—which had grown to number in the thousands—and Guardsmen clashed in pitched battles. As the Guardsmen were wildly outnumbered and generally disinclined to fire on American citizens, they suffered dozens of injuries and were forced to retreat to the county jail and fortify it to protect themselves and other members of law enforcement.

The mob eventually learned that Hughes had been placed in the District Attorney's second-story vault and set about laying hold of him. By 4 p.m., the courthouse was gutted by the fire, but the vault was still standing. The mob repeatedly but unsuccessfully placed dynamite (utilizing ladders) to open the vault door and then employed it in conjunction with cuts to the outer casing by an acetylene torch. Later that evening a blast finally blew in the vault door and Hughes was discovered freshly dead from suffocation or the final dynamite blast (one account indicated that part of his head was smashed in). Hughes' lifeless form was dropped down one of the ladders and struck the ground with a dull thud.

Members of the mob tied a chain around Hughes' body, affixed the chain to an automobile and dragged him "down to niggertown." The gruesome cavalcade ended at a tree near a two-story office building which housed several African American businesses, including a drug store, a beauty shop, an undertaker and a tailor. Hughes' body was hung from the tree and vigilantes piled up boxes underneath it. The mob set the boxes on fire and burned Hughes' body; then they burned down the African American office building. A reinforcement of Guardsmen arrived at approximately 2 a.m. and the mob dispersed.

On Saturday, May 10, images of the mob, the riot and the courthouse fire appeared in newspapers across Texas and the nation. Just after dawn, the Rangers and Guardsmen cut down Hughes' remains and sent them to a white undertaker (as the African American undertaker's parlor had been torched) and then sought out the hundreds of black citizens who had fled into the surrounding thickets, hidden under homes or otherwise taken refuge. The Guardsmen transported them back to the African American section of the community.

According to the *Fort Worth Star-Telegram*, "not a negro was seen in the town from 2 p. m. Friday until Saturday daybreak, although Sherman claimed a negro population of 1,500 to 2,000." When the returning African Americans and their escort got back to their neighborhood, they discovered typewritten ultimatums warning black

After members of a Sherman mob burned down the Grayson County Courthouse to get to George Hughes, they retrieved his corpse from the ruins and burned it to a crisp. *Image © Bettmann/CORBIS.*

citizens to leave the city within twenty-four hours.

Fifteen suspected mob participants were arrested and several injured National Guardsmen were transferred to a Dallas hospital. As further rioting was expected, state officials ordered additional Guardsmen to Sherman and these reinforcements were supplemented by almost fifty law enforcement personnel from surrounding counties. A Fort Worth contingent, for example, was utilized to protect the main school and church in the African American section of Sherman and set up machine gun positions at vantage points on streets leading to these locations. Guardsmen prohibited white citizens from entering black neighborhoods without specific, approved permission.

The *Star-Telegram* would later refer to the rioting the night before as an "orgy" of violence and destruction, and Sherman Mayor J. S. Eubank[34] would blame it on outsiders, claiming "Sherman has been made a victim of circumstance."

At 10:45 p.m. on May 10, Governor Moody declared a state of martial law in Sherman after noting that "reputable citizens and officers, including Judge R. M. Carter, have reported to me that the mob threatens to form again," further endangering the safety and security of the community.

By May 11, Guardsmen were posted with machine guns at the county jail and every corner of the courthouse square. They began patrolling the city and forbade the congregation of more than three citizens at a time on any city street.

On Monday, May 12, a military court began conducting a probe into the rioting, gathering testimony that would be used when the Grayson County grand jury convened the following week.

On Tuesday, May 20, the grand jury indicted fourteen suspects in seventy counts of five separate offenses, including rioting, rioting to commit arson, utilizing explosives to commit arson, rioting to commit murder and burglary of the courthouse—no one was indicted in the death of George Hughes.

The Sherman citizens charged were Jimmie Arnold, C. E. Briggs, Leslie Cole, Jeff (Slim) Jones, Jim May, J. B. McCasland, Alvin Morgan, Horace Reynolds, Bill Sofey and Cleo Wolfe. Four other men from Van Alstyne were charged: Roy Allen, Leonard (Baldy) O'Neal, Webb Purdom and Jess Roper. The bond for every suspect was set at $5,000 and their cases were transferred to Dallas County for trial.

On Saturday, May 24, martial law ended at noon and the Sherman rioting suspects were transferred to a Dallas jail. On May 27, federal charges alleging a civilian attempt to disarm national guardsmen was filed against Sherman residents John Edwards, Will Hamilton and Floyd Sheppard and Waxahachie resident John Simmons, each man's bond being set at $2,000. Hamilton and Edwards immediately posted bond and the officials of Grayson County filed a $100,000 insurance claim on the courthouse even though the policy the county carried on the courthouse contained a disclaimer invalidating recompense in the case that the edifice was destroyed by rioting.

On June 23, 1930, Dallas County District Court Judge Charles A. Pippen denied a plea to reduce the bond set for the Sherman riot defendants and postponed the trial until September. By early September, ten of the riot defendants had posted the $5,000 bonds, leaving only Arnold, McCasland, Morgan and Wolfe in Dallas County custody. On September 10, Judge Pippen announced that the hearings for the Sherman riot defendants would commence on September 29. On September 26, Judge Pippen postponed the hearings until November because the Grayson County District Attorney was busy with several other cases.

When the Sherman riot trial began, Defense Attorney J. A. Carlisle filed two separate motions to postpone the case again and transfer the hearings back to Grayson County. Judge Pippen overruled both motions and then had a disheartening encounter with an ugly Dallas County mindset.

Of the sixty-eight prospective jurors interviewed for the trial, sixty—almost 90%—declared openly that they would not convict the defendants even if the State demonstrated their guilt beyond a reasonable doubt. Attributing prospective juror prejudice to the publicity the riot had received, Judge Pippen noted that Dallas County sentiment "is overwhelmingly against the State's case without regard to the facts or guilt of those engaged in violation of the law" and transferred the hearings to the Travis County District Court.

J. B. McCasland's arson trial commenced in Austin in June of 1931 and he was convicted in a matter of weeks. In July he pled guilty to a charge of rioting and the three other charges against him were dismissed. McCasland was sentenced to two years for each offense, and the sixty-six cases against the other defendants were then transferred to Cooke County (Gainesville).

In Gainesville, County Attorney William C. Culp asked for a dis-

1930

Image of the Grayson County Courthouse after it was torched by its own citizens. *Dallas Morning News*, 1930.

missal of the indictments against Roy Allen, Jimmie Arnold, C. E. Briggs, Leslie Cole, Jim May, Alvin Morgan, Leonard (Baldy) O'Neal, Horace Reynolds, Bill Sofey and Cleo Wolfe because he believed the evidence against them was insufficient to ensure a conviction. The court agreed and released all ten. Cases against remaining defendants Jeff Jones, Webb Purdom and Jess Roper were scheduled for January 1932.

On June 3, 1932, the indictments against Jones, Purdom and Roper were dismissed (due to insufficient evidence) by Cooke County Judge Ben W. Boyd. It is unclear what became of the federal charges against Edwards, Hamilton, Sheppard and Simmons.

1933

Although no mass action against Negroes in the United States as a whole has ever been taken, it is none the less true that what the Jews in Germany are going through is very much akin to what negroes here have suffered lo, these many years. They have been exploited, mobbed, burned at the stake, strung from the first convenient tree-limb, and murdered in cold blood during beastly riots. Negroes in the United States are not economically situated so that any enormous fines could be assessed against them as was the case of the German Jews, but many an individual Negro has had to pay in money or forced labor a big price for petty crimes, that in many cases he did not commit. The German Jews have the edge on the Negroes of the world, however, in that all Negroes really know what it means to be persecuted and thus they sympathize with the Jews; and, too, the Jews seemingly have the sympathy of the whole world—except the Nazis—but who has any sympathy for the Negro unless it is God? True, there are many individuals among the majority who act as a buffer, and through their humane and just dealings, see that Negroes get some semblance of justice that is due every American citizen, but in the main, to be a Negro is to be a subject, at any time, to gross injustice and discrimination.

J. W. Aitch
San Antonio Register
November 18, 1938

The remains of an African American man named David Gregory were incinerated in a vacant lot in a black neighborhood in Kountze, Texas on December 7, 1933.

On Saturday, December 2, a thirty-year-old white woman named Nellie Williams Brockman left her and her husband's farm and headed to a department store in Kountze by truck. Somewhere along the way she ran into some type of trouble and was apparently shot. They found her body next to the truck and both the vehicle and her corpse were partially burned.

After Brockman's body was discovered, a few folks claimed they had seen a shotgun-wielding black man head into the woods not far from where the crime was committed. Local law enforcement officials mounted an intensive search for the suspect, utilizing platoons of armed volunteers and keen bloodhounds, but turned up nothing.

A few days into the manhunt, the Kountze Police Department became interested in an ex-con named David Gregory. According to the *San Antonio Express*, Gregory, a preacher's son, only became a suspect after a secret tip: "Cloaking their investigation in secrecy, officers said the tip was of such nature that to divulge it would greatly jeopardize chances of apprehending the fugitive."

The *Galveston Daily News* indicated that the tip came after Gregory was suspected and that it's source was one of the suspect's aunts. Whatever the case, when Gregory learned that he was a suspect, he disappeared and at least six African American men (including Gregory's brother) were arrested in an attempt to determine his location. The *Daily News* suggested that the informer placed Gregory at an African American church in the small community of Voth (now part of the northwest section of Beaumont, just east of U.S. Hwy 96 and the Pine Island Bayou).

On December 7, Hardin County Sheriff Miles D. Jordan, Sr., Deputy Sheriff Ralph B. Chance, Jefferson County Sheriff W. W. "Bill" Richardson and Deputy Sheriff Homer French headed to Voth and discovered Gregory at the described church, apparently concealed in the belfry. When they asked him to come down he refused and "flourished" a pistol (not a shotgun, the weapon the black suspect was reported carrying near the crime scene). Deputy Chance subsequently felled Gregory with a shotgun blast, the buckshot tearing into Gregory's face and neck and rendering him unconscious.

Sheriff Jordan *et al* took custody of Gregory and immediately transported him to a Beaumont Hospital. He was in critical condition and received emergency treatment, but the doctors indicated that he probably wouldn't survive till morning.

Sheriff Jordan had hoped Gregory would regain consciousness so the investigation could record his statement, but less than two hours after their arrival at the hospital, word was received that a mob had formed in Kountze and was headed towards Beaumont.

Hospital authorities expressed their discomfort with harboring a suspect that could put the facility at risk and Sheriff Jordan calculated that their chances at keeping Gregory from the mob were slim, in or outside the hospital.

Sheriff Jordan and the others snuck Gregory down a back elevator and placed him in Jordan's vehicle. Jordan, Richardson and French (in two separate cars) eluded the mob and drove east towards Vidor (seven miles east of Beaumont), planning to double-back and take Gregory to a hospital in Port Arthur (thirty miles farther south). Gregory never regained consciousness and died not long after the sheriff's car crossed into Orange County. Sheriff Richardson and Deputy French returned to Beaumont and Jordan pressed on.

Newspaper image of the African American church in Voth where David Gregory was gunned down. *Beaumont Journal*, 1933.

1933

As a mob was out and in force, Sheriff Jordan was not exactly sure what to do with Gregory's body. He considered a return to Beaumont unwise, so he turned and drove to Silsbee (twenty-three miles north/northwest). At Silsbee another mob had assembled and the local undertaker, fearing trouble, refused to accept Gregory's remains. Members of the Silsbee mob confronted the sheriff, but he convinced them to let Gregory's body remain in his custody.

With limited options and operating under the assumption that the Kountze mob was still in Beaumont, Sheriff Jordan headed back west. When he entered the Kountze community, an imposing throng of men crowded in front of his vehicle. As reported in the *Corsicana Daily Sun*, Jordan described the scene thusly:

> It was a sea of faces of silent but grimly determined men. I guess I might have got part of the way through by running over and killing a bunch of white men. I wasn't going to do that to save a dead negro who was guilty of a most revolting crime.

As Sheriff Jordan would later put it, he was "one against four hundred," and the four hundred seized Gregory's corpse and tied it to the back of an automobile. A fifty-car parade of white men then dragged the body around Kountze for close to an hour, so long that a large bonfire that had been lit to incinerate Gregory's remains burned out.

Denied a fire, the mob (according to the *Orange Leader* of Orange, Texas) "mutilated the body horribly in a savage demonstration of its spirit" (several accounts—including that of the *Houston Chronicle*--suggest Gregory's heart was cut out and a 1972 account indicated it was nailed to a tree on Main Street) and then re-fastened it to a car and "bounced" the body through the African American section of Kountze, reportedly screaming "Nigger for breakfast!" Members of the mob then delivered the mangled corpse to the front doorstep of Gregory's mother, whom they summoned.

Mrs. Gregory appeared and succinctly denied the mob her anticipated hysterics. She glanced over what was left of her dead son and said "You've done it right, white folks," and went back inside.

The white folks retrieved the hide-less grotesquery and dragged it to a new bonfire that had been built in a vacant lot not far from Gregory's home. The conflagration was constructed of fencing removed from neighboring African American yards and as Gregory's remains cooked, some members of the mob drank coffee and ate sandwiches. Several others started towards the jailhouse to lynch some of the other black men in custody. Sheriff Jordan met the vigilantes out front and informed them that the facility was well-protected and that they would have to go through him and his men first, so the smaller mob reconsidered or just ran out of steam.

The following morning, African Americans who passed by the smoking embers of the lynching pyre were reportedly called over to "see what happened to David Gregory." Some Texas newspapers included a photo of Gregory's remains smoldering in their May 8 reporting.[35]

By afternoon, the white citizens of Kountze had grown concerned about the possibility of African American retaliation or "up-

A curled scratch in the bottom center of this newspaper image indicates the smoking remains of David Gregory. In the *Beaumont Journal* version a crude arrow is drawn in the background to indicate the home of Gregory's mother. *Nolan County News*, 1933.

rising," so Kountze law enforcement personnel went through the black neighborhoods confiscating guns and knives. They stored the confiscated items at a local store until white trepidation passed.

Several years after the Gregory lynching, a local white man confessed to the murder of Nellie Williams Brockman on his deathbed.

Conclusion

Many African Americans were lynched around here, probably some in Grand Saline: hanged, decapitated and burned, some while still alive. The vision of them haunts me greatly. So, at this late date, I have decided to join them by giving my body to be burned, with love in my heart not only for them but also for the perpetrators of such horror...[36]

                         Charles Robert Moore
                         retired Methodist minister
                         suicide note
                         June 23, 2014

Early in the process of writing this book, a retired Caucasian man named Charles Robert Moore committed an act of self-immolation in East Texas.

By all accounts, Moore was a man of conscience and conviction. As a former Methodist minister in Austin, Moore participated in over 100 protests against the death penalty and once went on a hunger strike to challenge discriminatory language in the literature of the United Methodist Church. He traveled in India, Africa and the Middle East and was not afraid to challenge his beliefs. And he was steadfastly committed to defending the rights of others. As one colleague put it, "If you were ever on the side of powerlessness, if you were ever on the margins yourself and looking for someone to help you, Charles was the person."

In his retirement—at an age when most folks relaxed and contented themselves with sitting back and simply enjoying the time they had left—Moore was still mindful of injustice. He thought back to his youth in East Texas. He lamented the discrimination and persecution that African Americans there had experienced at the hands of their white neighbors and wondered if he had done enough

Conclusion

A depiction of an African American man burned at the stake. *Frank Leslie's Illustrated Newspaper*, 1868.

about it. He was haunted by this question.

Though his existence was characterized by courageous stances and an adherence to the principles of righteous opposition, Moore was troubled by the possibility of his own adolescent apathy and/or inaction—what most of us would consider a forgivable dalliance of youth. He wanted to bring attention to the atrocities that African Americans in his community suffered and the continued disempowerment and marginalization that they endure to the present day.

On June 23, 2014, Moore drove to his hometown of Grand Saline and parked his car in a Dollar General parking lot on East Garland Street. He lingered there momentarily and placed a foam mat on the ground. He knelt down on the mat and poured gasoline over his head and torso. Then he lit a match and burst into flame.

As Moore stood up and began to scream, two men rushed over and extinguished the blaze. He was transported to Parkland Hospital, but succumbed to his burns later that day.

After Charles Robert Moore killed himself, his relatives found a note that conveyed the sense of urgency he felt regarding the issue he died for: "I would much prefer to go on living and enjoy my beloved wife and grandchildren and others, but I have come to believe that only my self-immolation will get the attention of anybody and perhaps inspire some to higher service."

Moore's hometown newspaper's response to his act was to describe him as a troubled old man. The *Tyler Morning Telegraph* reported his self-immolation under a headline that read "Madman or

Martyr? Retired minister sets self on fire, dies." The story of Moore's suicide made the *Morning Telegraph*, the *Longview News-Journal*, the *Dallas Morning News*, the *Washington Post* and a few others, but his death did not draw widespread, serious news coverage or attract substantial attention to the history and issues he was disturbed by.

This book was not written to bring attention to Moore's death or justify his final act of protest. This book was written to bring light to a specific, demonstrable campaign of holocaust that spanned at least two generations of Texans at the turn of the 20th century and simply notes that Charles Robert Moore was one of the few white folks in Texas history who ever attempted to bring a discussion of this pattern of atrocity to the fore.

A recent study on American lynchings documented almost 4,000 African American victims in a dozen southern states (including Texas) between 1877 and 1950.[37] That works out to just over one lynching a week for three-quarters of a century. The discussion in this book notes five prior to 1877 and there is no doubt there were hundreds (if not thousands) more, but this effort is not a catalog of all the gruesome lynchings black Americans suffered during that period in the South. This effort is a compendium on one vile method whites in Texas utilized towards persons of color to terrorize them and maintain, ritualize and celebrate white sovereignty.

It is important to note and discuss the lynchings of African Americans that involved a noose, but white citizens also suffered the lynching noose—not at the frequency or extent that black citizens did, but it was not unheard of. Burnings at the stake were almost exclusively reserved for persons of color. And, again, between 1891 and 1922, an average of over one person of color a year met that horrendous fate and all but one were African American and most met their ends in East Texas—where Charles Robert Moore grew up and spent much of his life.

On November 22, 1903, an African American man nicknamed "Jack Cocoanut" was burned to death in Austin, Texas.

Background information was scarce, but Cocoanut had reportedly been "charged with lunacy" and was one of the six mentally handicapped persons residing at the Travis County jail at the time (awaiting placement in the overcrowded Texas State Lunatic Asylum). Cocoanut had apparently been an itinerant or teenaged foundling and was given his nickname because his "demented" condition rendered jail personnel unable to ascertain his real identity.

Early reports on Cocoanut's demise suggested that "in some mysterious way his clothing caught on fire and he was badly burned before being discovered." But on November 25 three African Americans (Sid Perry, Alex Teel and Oscar Redding) were charged in Cocoanut's death after an investigation suggested that the "insane boy" was "saturated with kerosene and a match applied." On December 2, a Grand Jury indicted Alex Teel and Oscar Redding (who had both been accused of robbery and were awaiting trial) for Cocoanut's murder. The two were tried and convicted in early March of 1904 and sentenced to twenty-five years in the state penitentiary on March 12.

Several aspects of this incident raise questions. First, it seems unlikely that any inmates (and especially African American inmates) in the Travis County jail at that time would have had ready access to kerosene and matches. Second, it can be safely assumed that most of the guards at the Travis County jail were white and that they probably did have ready access to kerosene and matches. And third, it is unlikely that the racial slur that the victim acquired as a nickname surname originated from his fellow African American prisoners.[38]

Considering these points, it seems counterintuitive that black inmates (who probably did their best to stick together in that prison setting) would have burned one of their own. In fact, if the jail was run by whites and reasonably populated with whites (Remember: a significant percentage of African Americans suspected or convicted of crimes—especially serious crimes—never made it to a courthouse, much less a jail.), the official storyline invites suspicion. But neither racism nor a racial norm establishes white motive and a lack of easy access to matches and kerosene doesn't eliminate the black suspects. The possibility of an African American man burning another African American man is simply disturbing, and the horrific death of "Jack Cocoanut" is a sad, suspicious tragedy in a long line of tragedies and crimes endured by African Americans—specifically in regards to fire. The cruel, insufferable irony permeating every detail of Cocoanut's death is that Teel and Redding, both black men, seem to be the only suspects ever indicted, prosecuted and found guilty (much less punished) for burning an African American alive in Texas. And this after decades of white men burning black men alive in broad daylight and detailed in the pages of major newspapers across the country!?

That the death of Jack Cocoanut begs speculation goes without saying; but even if Teel and Redding were innocent, it is important to remember that it might have been impossible for them to demonstrate their innocence or avoid conviction if innocent. With only a handful of exceptions, African Americans in Texas weren't permitted to serve on juries until the mid-1960s; and this means that Texas blacks were systematically denied the full measures of due process because they were unable to have their cases or complaints heard before citizens who legitimately comprised a jury of their peers. Formal and informal methods of justice were tilted against them and, if they weren't lynched informally by white vigilantes, they could certainly and were certainly often lynched formally by white judiciaries.

The odds are clearly against African Americans in the present judicial system (in terms of disproportionality of those convicted, incarcerated and/or executed), but the situation was worse in the early 20th century. Whites could jump to conclusions in terms of guilt without objection. Whites could be manipulative, mistaken or malicious in considerations of innocence and guilt and suffer no legal or ethical repercussions. Whites could (and inarguably did) blame or frame African American citizens for crimes perpetrated by whites themselves and then bolster the case against black stand-ins and shamelessly watch as their victims were falsely blamed and punished (officially, unofficially and/or extra-judicially). And whites could openly and brazenly defy and break laws and commit crimes that persons of color were beaten, banished or burned at the stake for.

Immediately following the Paris lynching of Henry Smith, several newspapers and newspaper editorialists made the case that any brute who committed the type of crime that Smith allegedly had, white or black, would "be ushered through the gates of the damned" in the same manner in which Smith was dispatched. The *Austin Statesman* proclaimed that "every true man in the South would rather die than yield one iota of his right to visit dire and terrible vengeance upon the brute or brutes who desecrate and humiliate the purity of Southern homes" and said to let the Smith lynching be "a lesson to the brutes, white or black, who touch with unhallowed hand the women of the country." And the *San Antonio Express* observed that "the Paris episode will strike a healthy terror to the cowardly hearts of beasts, both white and black, that prey on innocence." In point of fact, however, this "white or black" equation was strictly for show, presumably concocted to in some way justify the atrocities that had been committed or at least suggest that applying the torch was not racially motivated.

There is only one documented account of a white man being burned at the stake in Texas, and he reportedly met his fate at the hands of other white men exercising their right to visit "dire and terrible vengeance" upon Abolitionists. The incident reportedly occurred in Buchanan, Texas (a community that no longer exists), five miles northwest of present-day Cleburne. The account was gathered from telegraph communications and published in the *Cleveland Daily Leader* on May 16, 1860.[39] In the report (which the *Daily Leader* claimed was "kept out of the public prints" in Texas), a young, unidentified white man who was peddling Bibles, religious works, school materials and "unfortunately for him, a few copies of the 'Impending Crisis,'[40] and some tracts favoring the cause of Freedom," made the mistake of catching the attention of some "Pro-Slaveryites":

> A mob soon had him in their clutches, and he was at once unmercifully flogged, and robbed of his wagon and his contents. Here, perhaps, the affair would have ended, but at this juncture a negro man was brought upon the ground, purporting to have been caught running away from his master with a forged free pass in his pocket; he, the negro, was henceforth lashed to a tree, and after a most barbarous beating, he was told to say who had given him the pass.

"Well knowing who his captors wished him to accuse," the black runaway pointed at the young white man, and the young white man's fate was decided by an "infuriated mob, now numbering about 150 owners of slaves, their overseers and sons":

> These rolled the wagon under a tree, covered it with dry faggots, and over the whole of it poured a barrel of tar; having first stripped their victim and immersed him in the same, they passed

a rope around his neck and over a limb. Then, raising him so that his toes barely touched the top of the combustible pile, the negro was made to apply the burning torch, and thus the fearful tragedy closed in the flames of the hellishly concocted funeral pile,

The sexual abuse and assault of black women in the South was a matter of white male privilege. The animal lust that white men constantly accused black men of exhibiting in regards to white women, was actually indulged in a thousand fold more often by white men on black women--but white men suffered little or no consequences for their sexual criminality. *"Lovers" by Ernest Crichlow (1838) Image © The Metropolitan Museum of Art.*

and the shrieks of the agonized victim.

There are some accounts that suggest that indigenous North Americans may have burned a small number of Anglos alive, but it was often the other way round. In fact, there are several cases of American children mimicking their elders and accidentally burning playmates at the stake while playing "Cowboys and Indians."[41]

During the same period that whites were burning black men for allegedly desecrating "the purity of Southern [white] homes," there were white men who desecrated or violated the same notions of the purity or sanctity of Southern white homes and never faced the torch. And a substantial percentage of white men—on a larger scale than has ever been admitted—frequently violated the purity or sanctity of Southern black homes.

Raping black women without consequence in the South was a matter of white privilege; and this might explain why so many white men were so rabidly intent on burning black men for alleged sexual contact or sexual transgressions with white women. The thought of white women bearing the consequences of their father's, husband's, brother's or son's savagery or, perhaps worse, black men indulging themselves with white men's sisters, mothers or daughters in the same way white men exorcised their libidinal "demons" with recourse-less black women, was horrifying, maddening and unbearable. It made white perpetrators hysterical.

The possibility that the ritual incineration of black men was perhaps a subconscious attempt by guilty white men to annihilate their own sin or obliterate the memory of their criminal lust and diminished humanity is worth consideration. And it's clear that burning black men comprised a monstrous, vile, existential point of no return. Once Southern white men reduced themselves to holocaust, they descended into a moral and spiritual abyss lest they convince themselves that their victims were fiends, devils and brutes, subhuman "others" that had to be punished and executed shockingly. The resultant, ongoing barbarity comprised a twisted, socio-political manifesto etched in charred human flesh, an insane regimen of terrorism and, quite possibly, an abhorrent, sickening manner of catharsis. And when burnings at the stake fell out of fashion, white folks were perfectly eager to forget, misremember or bury this history, as if it didn't define their towns, linger in their communities and pervade every facet of their cultural soul, even to the present day.

These atrocities were never isolated incidents, and if you go to most of the communities where black holocausts were perpetrated (and those responsible went unpunished), you'll find a significant percentage of the citizenry still (at some level) invested in the inhumanity and racism related to the burnings long past. The rationalizations were handed down, the gleeful accounts shared; the innate capacity for monstrosity is still there.

Image of an African American man who met his fate at the hands of "Judge Lynch." *El Paso Daily Herald*, 1900.

Paris, Waco, Tyler, Greenville, Sherman, Texarkana, Sulphur Springs—Grand Saline—terror enjoyed refuge in these communities and they should acknowledge these egregious acts and formally remember the victims.

Slavery was a repulsive, indelible disgrace. The Civil War—like most conflicts foisted on us today—was a farce perpetrated on rank and file Southerners by the plantation-owning aristocracy.

Reconstruction was a bitter pill and Jim Crow was a psychotic Dixieland revival and sad continuance of devastating ignorance and depraved humanity. But bridging Reconstruction and Jim Crow was an era of white rage and black cinder that enforced the myth of white supremacy and deformed race relations in ways that reverberate to the present day. Some of the men of color burned at the stake were probably guilty, yes; but many were innocent, in love or in the wrong place at the wrong time. The horrendous ends they suffered—whether guilty or innocent—demean every precept of American justice and decency and render atonement or redress virtually unachievable.

When the citizens of Kirven watched Johnnie Cornish dive

head-first into his involuntary funeral pyre and deeply inhale red hot coals, how did they not recoil in utter, unshakable horror? When Henry Smith, innocent or guilty, "rubbed his eyeless sockets with the stumps of his arms," how did the surrounding throng keep from shrinking away, retching or slouching home to pray for their very being?

The participants in these acts of terror—the executioners and the onlookers—were degenerate rabble estranged from their own humanity.

The questions this period of holocaust raises are as immutable as the screams of the victims must have been. The wholesale cruelty is disturbing in ways that recall Nazi Germany, the Khmer Rouge or the genocide in Darfur. Except this malignance didn't happen in some far off killing field or concentration camp; it happened here. Texas doesn't bear the stigma, but—like most of the South (and, perhaps, America, in general)—it should.

In the current socio-political moment, forgetfulness is essentially a form of entitlement and benefactors of this self-conferred grace bristle at threats to their amnesia; but the luxury of misremembering is no longer an option. If the malignance was in remission, there are certainly portents of its return.

Black Holocaust

List of Known Persons of Color Who Were Burned at the Stake in Texas

List Compiled by Author

NAME	DATE	RACE	MUNICIPALITY/LOCATION	ALLEGED CRIME	RESULT
"Green"	09/08/1861	Black	Harrison County—Near Marshall	Rape/Murder	Burned
"Rube"	04/??/1863	Black	Southeast of Paris—Lamar County	Murder	Burned at the Stake
Unidentified Men (2)	02/16/1867	Black	Near Alabama Landing—Leon County	Freedmen	Burned
Anthony Smith	01/28/1876	Black	Cameron—Milam County	Murder	Burned at the Stake
John Joiner	12/13/1890	Black	Kerens Jail—Navarro County	Unknown	Burned
Lee Wilson	10/26/1891	Black	Douglassville—Cass County	Murder	Burned at the Stake
Ed Coy	02/20/1892	Black	Texarkana	Rape	Burned at the Stake
Henry Smith	02/01/1893	Black	Paris—Near Train Depot	Rape/Murder	Tortured/Burned
Henry Hillard	10/29/1895	Black	Tyler—Courthouse Square	Rape/Murder	Burned at the Stake
John Henderson	03/13/1901	Black	Corsicana—Courthouse Square	Murder	Burned at the Stake
Abe Wildner	08/21/1901	Black	Grayson Co—Red Branch	Rape/Murder	Hanged over a Fire
Dudley Morgan	05/22/1902	Black	Lansing Switch—Harrison County	Rape/Assault	Burned at the Stake
"Jack Cocoanut"	11/22/1903	Black	Austin	Lunacy	Burned
Tom Williams	08/11/1905	Black	Sulphur Springs	Rape/Assault	Burned at the Stake
Steve Davis	09/07/1905	Black	Howard—Ellis County	Rape/Assault	Burned at the Stake
Ted Smith	07/28/1908	Black	Greenville—Public Square	Rape	Burned at the Stake
Anderson Ellis	03/07/1909	Black	Rockwall	Assault	Burned at the Stake
Leonard Johnson	06/23/1910	Black	Lone Star—Cherokee County	Rape/Murder	Burned at the Stake
Henry Gentry	07/22/1910	Black	Belton—Courthouse Square	Murder	Dragged/Burned
Antonio Rodriguez	11/03/1910	Hispanic	Near Rock Springs—Edwards County	Murder	Burned at the Stake
Dan Davis	05/25/1912	Black	Tyler	Rape/Assault	Burned at the Stake
Will Stanley	07/31/1915	Black	Temple	Murder	Burned at the Stake
King Richmond	08/29/1915	Black	Sulphur Springs—Buford Park	Murder	Burned at the Stake
Joe Richmond	08/29/1915	Black	Sulphur Springs—Buford Park	Murder	Burned at the Stake
Jessie Washington	05/15/1916	Black	Waco—Heritage Plaza	Rape/Murder	Castrated/Burned
Bragg Williams	01/20/1919	Black	Hillsboro—Courthouse Square	Murder	Burned at the Stake
Ervin Arthur	07/06/1920	Black	Paris—Lamar County Fairgrounds	Murder	Burned at the Stake
Herman Arthur	07/06/1920	Black	Paris—Lamar County Fairgrounds	Murder	Burned at the Stake
Unidentified Man	??/??/1920	Black	Terrell Area—Kaufman County	Unknown	Burned
Alex Winn	08/15/1921	Black	Coolidge—Limestone County	Assault	Hanged/Burned
Wylie McNeely	10/10/1921	Black	Leesburg—Camp County	Rape	Burned at the Stake
Snap Curry	05/06/1922	Black	Kirven—Freestone County	Rape/Murder	Castrated/Burned
Johnnie Cornish	05/06/1922	Black	Kirven—Freestone County	Rape/Murder	Burned at the Stake
Mose Jones	05/06/1922	Black	Kirven—Freestone County	Rape/Murder	Burned at the Stake
Huley Owen	05/19/1922	Black	Texarkana	Murder	Shot/Burned
Joe Winters	05/20/1922	Black	Conroe—Courthouse Square	Rape	Burned at the Stake
Jesse Thomas	05/26/1922	Black	Waco—Downtown Plaza	Rape	Shot/Dragged/Burned
Jesse Davis	07/23/1924	Black	Dernal—Victoria County	Unknown	Burned at Bedpost
George Hughes	05/09/1930	Black	Sherman—Courthouse	Rape/Assault	Hanged/Burned
David Gregory	12/07/1933	Black	Kountze—Hardin County	Murder	Shot/Dragged/Burned

Endnotes

1. Smith's guilt was presumed from the very beginning and for the purpose of the narrative we will present the account from the prevailing perspective of the affirmative. As the incident never received a thorough investigation and the only suspect was denied due process, a full and complete record of the facts will probably never be known.

2. This report was reprinted in *The Facts in the Case of the Horrible Murder of Little Myrtle Vance and its Fearful Expiation at Paris, Texas, February 1, 1893*, an exculpatory account "Published for the Benefit of the Family of Henry Vance" and copyrighted by Henry Vance.

3. The phrase "caused from a rising" clearly suggested an injury resulting from Smith having stood up to or challenged a white man (or men). Whether the scar was the result of an altercation between Smith and Vance cannot be known, but the possibility should not be outside the realm of speculation.

4. A "G. M. Crook" was the sheriff of Lamar County in the early 1880s. When he lost a re-election bid to James H. Black on November 4, 1884, Crook and two of his deputies released a county prisoner with the agreement that he would kill Black. The prisoner killed Black and then later drowned while trying to cross an Arkansas river on a stolen horse. Crook's deputies were charged with Black's murder and turned state's evidence against him. Crook was prosecuted in Sherman but found not guilty.

5. Published in *The Facts in the Case of the Horrible Murder of Little Myrtle Vance and its Fearful Expiation at Paris, Texas, February 1, 1893*.

6. Besides Myrtle, a number of the Vance children (Eugene, Effie and John C.) died at early ages. Her older brother Beuford was the only Vance child to reach adulthood.

7. Beuford D. Vance (February 1, 1878 – December 16, 1949).

8. It should be mentioned that the city of New York was singularly qualified to lament "Another Negro Burned." Fifteen slaves were burned at the stake there after the farcical Slave Conspiracy Trial in 1741.

9. Governor Hogg's denunciation of the lynching and prosecutorial urgency in terms of holding the perpetrators accountable was probably not a bluff. After Lee Green was burned at the stake in Cass County fifteen months prior, Hogg was unequivocally condemnatory and offered rewards to bring those responsible to justice.

10. Dahomey was an African kingdom (located in the area of the present-day Benin) which lasted from about 1600 until 1904.

11. George Frisbie Hoar (August 29, 1826 – September 30, 1904) was a United States Senator from Massachusetts. He was an important critic of political corruption, took an early stand for Women's suffrage (in 1886) and fought for the rights of African Americans and Native Americans.

12. On September 9, 1892—less than four months before Henry Smith was burned at the stake in Paris—the *Dallas Morning News* mentioned Rube's lynching (noting the area had "a history") when it reported the lynch-mob hangings of three African American men, Bill Armor, John Ransom and Jack Walker.

After a black sharecropper named Jarett Burns was gunned down by a white man, a small white mob then attempted to lynch his niece, Ella Ransom. Armor, Walker, John Ransom and several other armed African Americans served as a protective escort for Ella, delivering her to Paris so she could report the attempted lynching to the proper authorities. This instance of black assertiveness angered many local white men and they decided to send a message. Three of the black men who guarded Ella received severe beatings; Armor, Walker and John Ransom were taken out into the woods and lynched, their bodies left hanging in the trees.

The *Morning News'* takeaway in mentioning the Rube lynching in relation to the contemporary triple lynching was the suggestion that things had changed in the Paris area and that the new outbreak of vigilante lawlessness was an unfortunate anomaly: "It is deplored by the good people as it places a stigma upon the good name of the county. . . if wise counsel prevails there will be no more of it." *The Morning News'* optimism in terms of the "good people" in the Paris area was obviously misplaced, and it is important to note that "A. McCuistion"—the assistant Lamar County attorney that Governor Hogg thirty years later urged to keep Smith away from Paris if a lynch-mob was forming—was surely a relation of Rube's alleged victim, Margaret McCuistion.

13. Charles Griffin (December 18, 1825 – September 15, 1867) was a career officer in the United States Army and a Union general in the Civil War. He rose to command a corps in the Army of the Potomac and served in many of the key campaigns in the Eastern Theater. After the war, he commanded the Department of Texas during Reconstruction. He was an ardent supporter of the Congressional policies of the Radical Republicans and freedmen's rights. He boldly and controversially disqualified a number of antebellum state officeholders in Texas, replacing them with loyal Unionists.

14. Andrew Sidney Broaddus (1810 – April 25, 1891) was a member of the Virginia House of Delegates from 1844-45 and piloted a mile-long wagon train of approximately 200 people to Texas in 1854. Later, serving as a stand-in, Broaddus debated Sam Houston in 1857 and served in Texas Secession Convention in 1861. He was a member of the Texas Legislature twice, from 1861-1863 and again in 1873. In 1868, while an attorney, Broaddus represented an African American woman named Phillis Oldham who had cohabitated with her owner, Major William Oldham, and borne him several children. When Major Oldham passed away, his white relatives tried to evict Phillis and her children from the Major's property, but Broaddus won her homestead property

End Notes

rights in the Burleson County Probate Court.

15. In most reports he is referred to as "Lee Wilson." The most localized news source that could be found to verify his identity was the *Alliance Standard* out of Linden, Texas. It referred to him as "Lee Green."

16. A trace chain is one of the two straps, ropes or chains by which a wagon is drawn by a harness animal.

17. The *Marshall News Messenger* later noted that Green may have had two accomplices; their names were listed as Louis Johnson and Jim Walker.

18. Almost six-and-a-half years later (June 2, 1898), an African American named Bud Hayden was hanged by a lynch-mob from the "limb of a tree which stood within a few feet of where Ed Coy was burned for a like offense" (*Atlanta Constitution*, June 4, 1898).

19. Albion Winegar Tourgée (May 2, 1838 – May 21, 1905) was an American soldier, politician, lawyer, judge and writer. A radical, late 19th-century civil rights activist, he founded the National Citizens' Rights Association, established Bennett College (an early black women's university) and is credited with introducing the metaphor of "color-blind justice" into legal discourse.

20, The description in terms of the suspect's exact shoe-size is suspicious. Did Mr. Caldwell glean this information during Wildner's alleged, short, initial visit earlier in the day? Was Wildner known to other parties familiar with the accusation? These aspects of specificity are at least mildly troubling and suggest that perhaps Mr. Caldwell (or another party involved) was much more familiar with Wildner than originally reported.

21. Arturo Alfonso Schomburg, also Arthur Schomburg (January 24, 1874 – June 8, 1938), was a Puerto Rican historian, writer, and activist in the United States. Schomburg increased the awareness of African American contributions to American society and was an important figure in the Harlem Renaissance. His collection of literature, art, slave narratives, and other materials of African American history became the basis for the Schomburg Center for Research in Black Culture at the New York Public Library branch in Harlem.

22. One report noted that Cherry was "the wealthiest negro in the city" and that he "was informed that his family would be protected until they could wind up their business affairs and leave." Successful African Americans of the period were not popular in East Texas and their wealth, prosperity and/or affluence comprised grounds for lynchings, massacres and racial expulsions on more than one occasion. See the author's previous offering, *The 1910 Slocum Massacre: An Act of Genocide in East Texas* (The History Press, 2014) for one example.

23. This was not uncommon in the South. A white man's assault of a black woman was not a crime; a black man's assault of a black woman was barely a crime. A black man's assault of a white woman was a death sentence.

In 1893 an African American man named Lewis Woods was found guilty of "ravishing a young colored girl" in Louisiana and imprisoned. In October 1893, he escaped and, within a week, had allegedly raped a white woman. Louisiana authorities tracked him to the Neches River in Texas and captured him there. Woods' captors boarded a train with him to Lake Charles, Louisiana, but the escort was confronted at Edgerly Station just after crossing the state line. Woods was seized immediately and burned at the stake for the rape of the white woman.

24. When Mexican President Porfirio Díaz resigned on May 25, 1911, Francisco León De La Barra served as interim president until November 6, 1911, when Francisco I. Madero was elected.

25. Mexico's claim for reparation was never addressed but another reparation claim was. After "justice in a more horrible form than that meted out to Henry Smith at Paris" was visited upon two Indians in Seminole Territory (J. Markus McGelsey and Palmer Simpson) by an Oklahoma mob on January 8, 1898, the Seminole tribe presented a claim for reparations to the U. S. Government. U. S. officials agreed to reparations and began making payments to the aggrieved parents and miscellaneous Seminole parties on February 14, 1899.

26. On April 30, 1909, at approximately 8 p.m., an eighteen-year-old white girl named Winnie Harmon was allegedly beaten and left in a barn just outside Tyler. Her brother discovered her a short time later and her attacker was described as an African American man with atypically dark skin.

Smith County Sheriff Wig Smith formed a posse and found a dark-skinned black man named Jim Hodges at another African American's house that same night, four and a half miles outside Tyler. When the posse tried to arrest Hodges, an older black man at the residence protested and threw an ax at Sheriff Smith—twice—but the sheriff and his posse were undeterred. They took Hodges into custody and transported him to the Smith County jail.

When Hodges was presented to Harmon the following morning, she wasn't sure he was her attacker. "I can't tell," she said. "I can't say he is the negro, but I can't say he is not the negro."

The facts notwithstanding, a white mob of thousands later surrounded the county jail and seized Hodges. The lynch-mob transported Hodges to the site of the new Smith County Courthouse (which was still under construction) and participants threw a rope up over an enormous derrick—that was being utilized at the site for hoisting large stones for the new courthouse—and fashioned a noose on one end. They placed the noose around Hodges' neck and several men took hold of the other end of the rope and jerked him into the sky.

Hodges squirmed and convulsed as he swung back and forth above the mob, and then his movements dwindled to a twitch or two before he grew still.

No one involved in the lynching attempted to conceal their identity and within ten minutes the construction site was empty, save the deceased, whose gruesome figure hung motionless in midair.

When Texas Governor Thomas Campbell received word of the Hodges lynching, he immediately dispatched a state militia to Tyler. On May 3, State Legislator Chester H. Terrell, of San Antonio, introduced a house resolution calling on the governor to submit a measure that required the criminal district court of Smith County to indict those involved in the lynching and, though Terrell's measure was predictably buried in committee and never revisited, there was an earnest attempt to prosecute the Hodges lynching. District Court Judge R. W. Simpson, Sheriff Smith and County Attorney Roy Butler conferred and over a dozen arrest warrants were issued.

Butler stated unequivocally that the evidence gathered in regards to the assault of Winnie Harmon did not implicate Hodges and that an innocent man had been lynched. On May 6, the names of the alleged lynchers were released and Judge Simpson began examining witnesses to secure grand jury indictments.

On July 1, after a special, eight-day session which included incriminating eyewitness testimony from a Smith County deputy sheriff, an all-white grand jury returned a no bill, concluding that the charges alleged in the indictments were not sufficiently supported by the evidence. Members of the lynch-mob were never punished and the cruel injustice of the Jim Hodges' lynching was never addressed.

27. Though Smallwood's two-volume, 840-page *Born In Dixie: The History of Smith County, Texas* (Eakin Press, 1998) was remiss in its failure to mention the burnings at the stake that occurred in Tyler at the end of the 19th and the beginning of the 20th centuries, it's discussion of the county during Reconstruction (titled "The County's Redeemers Win the War of Reconstruction") is honest and frank. Smallwood portrays the treatment of the local African American citizenry at the hands of white, "unreconstructed ex-Confederates" as a reign of terror.

28. The *Dallas Morning News, McKinney Courier-Gazette, San Antonio Express, Weatherford Weekly Herald*, etc., reported that Sheriff Butler and Deputy Flippin had approached King Richmond on a minor charge, but in *Texas Lawmen, 1900-1940: More of the Good and the Bad* (2012), Clifford R. Caldwell and Ronald G. Delord state that the charges against King also applied to his brother Joe and that they were major charges rather than minor ones. In point of fact, Caldwell and Delord misread the background information in the August 29 *Sulphur Springs Gazette* report on the lynching, completely missed the September 3 *Honey Grove Signal* report and, unfortunately, mistakenly claim that King and Joe had actually been charged with torching Sheriff Butler's house, stealing some of his horses and shooting his wife to death.

29. Calvin Maples Cureton (September 1, 1874 – April 4, 1940) would go on to serve as Chief Justice of the Texas Supreme Court from 1921-1940).

30. A Marshall, Texas native, Clifton Frederick Richardson, Sr. (October 30, 1892–August 1939) was an African American editor, publisher, journalist, political activist, and civic booster in Houston from the age of 19 until his death in 1939.

31. If Hardy Goodner Moore was correct, McGrew's role in the Arthur brothers capture may have earned him light sentences in at least two murder cases years later (the last of which involved the cold-blooded killing of his wife and stepdaughter). According longtime *Paris News* editor Alexander W. Neville (who practically lauded the Paris holocaust of Henry Smith twenty-seven years before the Arthur brothers faced the torch), McGrew "was for several years the most notorious character among his race in and about Paris, and caused more court action than ordinarily falls to one man."

McGrew was twice sentenced to the state penitentiary for murder, "each time being pardoned through the influence of white friends in Paris before the time his sentences expired." Also, it should be noted that B. B. Sturgeon–the Lamar County Attorney when Henry Smith was burned at the stake in Paris–later served as McGrew's defense attorney in at least one of his murder trials.

32. If dozens of African American men were burned to death in Texas from 1861-1933, hundreds (if not thousands) were lynched by noose and thousands if not tens of thousands (including men, women and children) were flogged, beaten or otherwise brutalized.

33. Texas Ranger Francis Augustus Hamer (March 17, 1884 – July 10, 1955) would later become known for his involvement in tracking down and killing Bonnie Parker and Clyde Barrow in 1934.

34. Though a Grayson County native, Jessie Shain Eubank (January 20, 1884 – June 7, 1942) was mayor of Corsicana from 1923-1925 before he served as mayor of Sherman.

35. It appeared in the December 14 edition of the *Nolan County News* (Sweetwater).

36. In his suicide note, Moore mentions an instance in his youth when a local Grand Saline man known as "Uncle Bill" boasted about the "niggers" he had killed and how he and others had placed their heads on poles. A section of Grand Saline was referred to as "pole town" for years and even a cursory examination of the community's history yields a chilling anecdote. The October 31, 1868 edition of *Flake's Semi-Weekly Bulletin* (Galveston) reported that a white doctor named Page was decapitated in the Grand Saline (formerly known as Jordan's Saline) area and his head was found hanging from a tree over a mile from his body. Dr. Page was decapitated because he dared treat black freedmen. Other accounts indicate Dr. Page's head was "hung from a pole" near the community instead of a tree.

37. "Lynching in America: Confronting the Legacy of Racial Terror," by the Equal Justice Initiative. This study chronicles EJI's investigation into lynching in twelve Southern states during the period between Reconstruction and World War II.

38. These days, the slur "coconut" denotes a black person who is accused of trying to act or be "white." In 1903, blacks were vigorously and systemically discouraged by whites from acting "white." The name "Cocoanut" implies chocolate+nut ("nut" as in "crazy" person) and probably originated in the mind of a clever racist in the Travis County jail's employ.

39. Mentions of the incident also appeared in other publications, including *The Liberator* in Boston, Massachusetts.

40. *The Impending Crisis of the South: How to Meet It* was a book self-published by North Carolinian Hinton Rowan Helper in New York, 1857. It comprised an early and cogent attack on slavery as a barrier to the economic advancement of whites in the South. Widely distributed by Horace Greeley and other prominent anti-slavery leaders, it infuriated the Southern aristocracy by suggesting that the South's *slavish*

reliance on slavery stunted its own economy by preventing economic development and industrialization, which, in turn, demonstrated why the South had progressed so much less than the North since the late 18th century. Framed more in terms of rational, white self-interest than altruism towards blacks (the author himself was surprisingly racist), Helper's insights were aimed at poor Southern whites, whom he claimed were being oppressed and misled by a small number of wealthy slave-owners. "Freesoilers and abolitionists are the only true friends of the South" Helper wrote. "Slaveholders and slave-breeders are downright enemies of their own section." Mere possession of *The Impending Crisis of the South: How to Meet It* could get you arrested or lynched in many parts of the South.

41. In 1923, eleven-year-old Charles Spindler and sixteen-year-old William Hubbard were burned at the stake in New Jersey during a game of "Indian Massacre." In 1935, a nine-year-old Massachusetts boy named Edward Smith was burned at the stake while playing "Cowboys and Indians." In 1967, Arthur Garcia was burned at the stake in San Antonio while playing "Cowboys and Indians" with two friends. They tied him to a post and placed some paper at his feet and then lit the paper. As one friend was trying to extinguish the flames, the other accidentally knocked over a can of paint thinner and the resulting explosion burned Garcia to death.

Bibliography

Abilene Daily Reporter. "Alleged Murderer Burned At the Stake." November 4, 1910.
_____. "Sheriff Believed at Least Two of Negroes Lynched Were Guilty." May 7, 1922.
_____. "Pioneer West Texas Preacher Has Vivid Memories of Civil War Days." January 22, 1945.
Abilene Semi-Weekly Farm Reporter. "Negro Burned At Stake." January 24, 1911.
_____. "Negro Will Stanley Burned." August 3, 1915.
_____. "Negro Was Known Here." August 3, 1915.
Aitch, J. W. "Called Home." *San Antonio Register*, Vol. 8, No. 33, November 18, 1938.
Akers, Monte. *Flames After Midnight: Murder, Vengeance, and the Desolation of a Texas Community*. Austin: University of Texas Press, 1999.
Albany News. "Judge Lynch in the North and South." August 23, 1901.
_____. "Burned at the Stake." June 24, 1910.
Albany Weekly News. "All Over the State." October 27, 1893.
_____. "Shooting near Paris." June 29, 1894.
Alliance Standard. "Proclamation." November 4, 1891.
_____. "Bunkum." November 17, 1891.
Alto Herald. "Negro Suspect at San Antonio." May 30, 1912.
Amarillo Daily News. "Fewer Lynchings in Year Just Closing." December 28, 1912.
_____. "Second Lynching in Mississippi." February 9, 1913.
Anaconda Standard. "Negro Fiend Burned at Stake in Texas." August 21, 1901.
_____. "How Wildner Died in Flames at Stake." August 22, 1901.
Arizona Republican. "Death by Fire." February 3, 1893.
Arlington Journal. "Greenville Negro Burned." July 31, 1908.
Atlanta Constitution. "Arkansas Mob Hangs a Negro," June 4, 1898.
_____. "Negro Is Burned in Public Square." January 21, 1919.
Aurora Daily Express. "Torture in Texas." February 2, 1893.
Austin Daily Herald. "Negro Burned at the Stake." September 6, 1905.
Austin Weekly Statesman. "Prepared for a Lynching." February 25, 1892.
_____. "Henry Smith Captured." February 2, 1893.
_____. "Vengeance Is Mine Saith the Lord." February 9, 1893.
_____. "Died By Fire." February 9, 1893.
_____. "Uphold Their Neighbors." February 16, 1893.
_____. "The Governor's Message." February 16, 1893.
_____. "Threaten Gov. Hogg." March 29, 1894.
Barr, Alwyn. *Black Texans: A History of African Americans in Texas.* Norman: University of Oklahoma Press, 1996.
Bastrop Advertiser. "Untitled." November 9, 1895.
_____. "The Negro, Abe Wildner." August 24, 1901.
Baylor Lariat. "Waco Is No Stranger to Grotesque Side of Life." October 25, 2013.

Bibliography

Belleville Daily Freeman. "Negro Burned at the Stake." September 8, 1905.
Beaumont Journal. "Kountze Quiet After Burning Negro's Body." December 8, 1933.
_____. "Negro's Guilt Is Undoubted." December 8, 1933.
_____. "Sheriff Tells Story of How Negro's Body Was Seized and Burned By Mob at Kountze." December 8, 1933.
Belvidere Daily Republican. "Southern Mob Burns Negro Over Slow Fire." October 11, 1921.
Boston Daily Globe. "Burned at Stake." February 2, 1893.
Boston Globe. "Mob Hangs Negro Who Shot Sheriff." April 23, 1918.
Boston Post. "White Savagery." February 2, 1893.
Breckenridge Daily American. "Negro Burned at Stake in Camp County." October 11, 1921.
Brenham Daily Banner. "A Negro Rapist Burned."February 23, 1892.
_____. "Texas Items." March 29, 1902.
Brenham Daily Banner-Press. "Sixth Lynching in Texas Within Month Reported." May 20, 1922.
Brooklyn Daily Eagle. "Negro Burned at Stake." March 13, 1901.
Brownsville Herald. "Indignation High." March 20, 1901.
_____. "Texas Troops Leave Sherman." May 25, 1930.
Brownwood Bulletin. "Negro Rapist Is Lynched By Georgia Mob." September 10, 1919.
_____. "Ranger Detachments Sent To Freestone County To Prevent Race War." May 8, 1922.
_____. "Seven Negro Men Lynched in Two Weeks." May 22, 1922.
_____. "Texas Leads South in Lynching Record for First Half of Year." June 30, 1922.
_____. "Authorities Deny Torturing Negro to Secure Confessions." February 13, 1923.
_____. "When Sanity Surprises." February 13, 1923.
_____. "Rushing Through Mighty Fast Says Convicted Slayer." March 29, 1923.
_____. "Waco Negro on Trial for Fifth Time During Past Two Weeks." March 30, 1923.
_____. "Grand Jury to Request Pardon for 2 Negroes." April 18, 1923.
Bryan Daily Eagle and Pilot. "Burned At The Stake for Assault." June 5, 1898.
_____. "Burned At The Stake." October 22, 1902.
_____. "Ravisher Soon Roasted." July 29, 1908.
_____. "Negro Convict Is Burned At Stake." October 5, 1910.
_____. "Negro Hurried Away from Angry Mob." May 27, 1912.
_____. "Thousands Witness Burning of Negro." July 31, 1915.
Buenger, Walter L. *Southwestern Historical Quarterly*, Vol. 103, July 1999 - April 2000.
Bullard, Sara, Ed. *Ku Klux Klan: A History of Racism and Violence*. Darby: Diane Publishing, 1998
Caldwell, Cliff and DeLord, Ron. *Texas Lawmen, 1835-1899: The Good and the Bad.* The History Press, 2011.
Cambridge Jeffersonian. "Vengeance." February 9, 1893.
Cameron Herald. "Is A Closed Incident." August 12, 1915.
_____. "Negro Lynched at Waco, Texas." May 18, 1916.
Canonsburg Weekly Notes. "The Craze for More Territory." February 10, 1893.
Cass County Sun. "Greenville Mob Burns Negro at the Stake." August 4, 1908.
Charlotte Observer. "Negro Burned at Stake." July 29, 1908.
Cleveland Daily Leader. "A Man Burned at the Stake in Texas." May 16, 1860.

Clifton Record. "Sank Majors Hanged by Mob." August 11, 1905.
_____. "Burned at the Stake." November 11, 1910.
_____. "Report Is Made on Hillsboro Lynching." February 28, 1919.
Coffeyville Daily Journal. "Mob Burns a Negro." October 11, 1921.
Colorado Citizen. Untitled. September 21, 1861.
Comanche Chief. "Triple Lynching Follows Brutal Murder." May 12, 1922.
Conroe Carrier. "A Mob Outwitted." October 17, 1902.
_____. "Buchanan is Dead." October 24, 1902.
Corpus Christi Caller. "Negro Burned At the Stake by Angry Mob. "October 12, 1921.
Corsicana Daily Sun. "Mexicans Are Giving Trouble." November 11, 1910.
_____. "Negro Burned at Hillsboro." January 21, 1919.
_____. "No Action On Motion." March 12, 1919.
_____. "Moody Aroused Over Sherman Mob Action; Guilty Be Punished." May 10, 1930.
_____. "Martial Law Is Still in Force Sherman Monday." May 19, 1930.
_____. "Alleged Rioters Cases Set Dallas for November 17." October 10, 1930.
_____. "Plea of Guilty in Sherman Mob Cases in Austin." July 2, 1931.
_____. "Final Sherman Riot Cases Dismissed at Gainesville Friday." June 3, 1932.
_____. "Negro Accused of Murdering White Woman Is Burned." December 8, 1933.
Corsicana Semi-Weekly Light. "Three Negroes Burned at Stake Saturday Morning at Kirven—Women Present." May 9, 1922.
_____. "Waco Quiet Today Following One of Wildest Days Seen in City's History—Negro Burned." May 26, 1922.
Courier Gazette. "Burned Up Is the Black Fiend." July 28, 1908.
_____. "Sunday Arrests." March 8, 1909.
_____. "Two Negroes Burned at Stake at Sulphur Springs; Killed Officers." August 30, 1915.
Daily Advocate. "Paris Is Ready For Them." February 14, 1893.
Daily Ardmoreite. "Negro Wildner Burned." August 21, 1901.
Daily Bulletin. "W. F. Bane, Acting Coroner." March 10, 1909.
_____. "Negro Murderer Burned At Stake." August 14, 1911.
Daily Concord Standard. "Burned at the Stake." May 23, 1902.
Daily Courier-Gazette. "Negro Burned at Rockwall." March 8, 1909.
Daily Express. "Indictment of Animals." July 24, 1908.
_____. "Greenville Mob Burns A Negro in Public Square." July 29, 1908.
_____. "Enraged Citizens Burn Mexican Who Kills a Woman." Nov. 10, 1910.
_____. "Oklahoma may Add Fuel to Ire of Mexicans." Nov. 14, 1910.
_____. "Suspect Killed; Waco Mob Burns Body." June 3, 1922.
Daily Free Press. "Negro Burned by Texas Mob." August 12, 1905.
Daily Hesperian. "Burned at the Stake." October 28, 1891.
_____. "Burned to Death." October 31, 1895.
Daily News. "A Sequel to the Paris Lynching." February 8, 1893.
Daily Northwestern. "Another Negro Burned." March 14, 1901.
Dallas Express. "Accused Was Sentenced to Hang February 21." January 25, 1919.
_____. "The Growing Menace of Mobocracy." February 1, 1919.
_____. "N.A.AC.P. Takes a Hand in Texas Lynching." February 1, 1919.
_____. "Lynching Must Go." March 15, 1919.
_____. "Hill County Grand Jury Fails to Return 'Lynching' Bills." July 19, 1919.
Dallas Morning News. "Burned at the Stake." October 27, 1891.

Bibliography

_____. "Coy Burned at the Stake." February 21, 1892.
_____. "The Triple Lynching." September 9, 1892.
_____. "An Atrocity in Lamar." January 28, 1893.
_____. "The Paris Horror." January 29, 1893.
_____. "Myrtle Vance Murder." January 31, 1893.
_____. "Capture of Smith." February 1, 1893.
_____. "Horror of Horrors." February 2, 1893.
_____. "The Paris Horror." February 3, 1893.
_____. "The State Press." February 9, 1893.
_____. "Hogg's Special Message." February 11, 1893.
_____. "Paris Burning." February 14, 1893.
_____. "The State Press." February 14, 1893.
_____. "Hogg's Special Message." February 15, 1893.
_____. "Paris Holocaust." February 16, 1893
_____. "Nugent on the Lynching." February 17, 1893.
_____. "The State Press." February 21, 1893.
_____. "Montgomery's Horror." August 3, 1893.
_____. "Roasted to Death." October 30, 1895.
_____. "Officers Hide Prisoner." March 9, 1901.
_____. "Taken from Train." March 13, 1901.
_____. "Burnt at Stake." March 14, 1901.
_____. "Negro Murderer Is Burned." August 21, 1901.
_____. "Agony Drawn Out." May 23, 1902.
_____. "Description of Execution." September 8, 1905.
_____. "Quick Vengeance Dealt to Negro." March 8, 1909.
_____. "The Main Excuses of the Lynchers." March 4, 1910.
_____. "Negro Is Burned to Death at Stake." June 21, 1910.
_____. "Negro Is Burned to Death at Stake." July 23, 1910.
_____. "Anti-American Demonstration." November 9, 1910.
_____. "Reparation for Lynching." November 10, 1910.
_____. "Flag Is Insulted by Mexican Mob." November 10, 1910.
_____. "Texas Governor Hears from Knox." November 12, 1910.
_____. "Armed Mexicans Reported on March." November 15, 1910.
_____. "Mexican Uprising Feared at Juarez." November 16, 1910.
_____. "Negro Meets Death at Stake in Tyler." May 26, 1912.
_____. "Will Stanley Burned at Stake in Temple." July 31, 1915.
_____. "Sulphur Springs Mob Burns Two Negroes." August 30, 1915.
_____. "Confession in Fryar Case Is Announced." May 10, 1916.
_____. "Jesse Washington Is Burned at the Stake." May 15, 1916.
_____. "Negro Is Burned to Death at Hillsboro." January 21, 1919.
_____. "Two Negroes Kill Father and Son." July 3, 1920.
_____. "Negro Who Killed Officer Is Burned." May 20, 1922.
_____. "Man Granted Bond on Lynching Charges." June 13, 1922.
_____. "Texarkana Lynching Trials Are Postponed." July 7, 1922.
_____. "Two Boys Burn to Death at Stake." August 28, 1923.
_____. "Klan Wizard Denies Charges." April 18, 1928.
_____. "Negro in Jail After Assault Near Sherman." May 4, 1930.
_____. "Mob Fails in Attempt to Get Negro in Jail." May 7, 1930.
_____. "Military Court Is Conducting Rioting Probe." May 13, 1930.
_____. "U.S. to Probe Mob Rioting at Sherman." May 15, 1930.

_____. "Indict 14 for Sherman Riot." May 21, 1930.
_____. "Sherman Mob Prisoners Put in Dallas Jail." May 24, 1930.
_____. "Grayson County Files Claim for Courthouse." May 28, 1930.
_____. "Attempt Made to Prove Alibi of McCasland." June 4, 1930.
_____. "Sherman Men's Trials Passed." June 24, 1930.
_____. "Sherman Riot Trials Fixed." September 10, 1930.
_____. "Grayson Attorney Busy, Riot Cases to Be Tried Later." September 10, 1930.
_____. "Sherman Cases Sent to Travis County." November 18, 1930.
_____. "Ten of Indictments in Riot Case Dismissed." November 3, 1931.
_____. "Frenzied Crowd Mutilates Body of Slain Negro." December 9, 1933.
_____. "Boy Burned at Stake While Playing Is Dead." March 11, 1935.
_____. "Game of Cowboys, Indians Blamed in Youth's Death." August 16, 1967.
Dallas Morning News. "In Dying Act, Minister Hoped to Inspire Social Justice." July 11, 2014.
Davenport Democrat. "K.K.K. Chief Denies Texas Negro Burned." April 13, 1928.
Decatur Evening Herald. "Fifteen Quizzed in Mob Killing." May 12, 1930.
The Democrat. Untitled. February 2, 1893.
_____. "A Horrible Sight." February 9, 1893.
_____. "The Statesman Speaks." February 23, 1893.
_____. "Burned at the Stake," November 7, 1895.
_____. "Burned the Black." May 29, 1902.
_____. "Burned at the Stake." August 17, 1905.
Denton Record-Chronicle. "Heavy Guard Protects Negroes in Texas Jail after Mob Burns Suspect." December 8, 1933.
Donaldsonville Chief. "Woman's Slayer Is Burned by Texans." December 24, 1910.
The Eagle. "Waco Public Square Scene of Execution." May 15, 1916.
Early, J. M. *An Eye for an Eye or The Fiend and the Fagot: An Unvarnished Account of the Burning of Henry Smith at Paris, Texas, February 1, 1893*. Marshall's Printing House.
El Paso Daily Herald. "Burned At Stake." October 20, 1899.
_____. "Grewsome Work of Judge Lynch." January 16, 1901.
_____. "Burned at the Stake." January 16, 1901.
_____. "Human Torch." August 29, 1901.
El Paso Herald. "Murderous Mobs at Henderson, Texas, Fall Sullenly Back." October 16, 1902.
_____. "Negro Is Burned at the Stake By a Mob in Texas." September 8, 1905.
_____. "Texas Mob Burns Negro." July 23, 1910.
_____. "Texans Burn Mexican Citizen of Mexico Who Killed Woman." October 4, 1910.
_____. "Sonora Paper Berates Yankees." November 17, 1910.
_____. "Negro Burned at Stake in Texas Town." May 25, 1912.
_____. "15,000 at Waco See Negro Burn." May 15, 1916.
_____. "Texas City Calm After Burning of Negroes." July 7, 1920.
_____. "Special Jury to Probe Lynching." July 10, 1920.
_____. "Another Negro Burned at Stake by a Texas Mob." October 11, 1921.
El Paso Herald-Post. "Negro's Body Burned by Mob." December 8, 1933.
El Regidor. "Otro Hecho Salvaje." November 2, 1895.
Emporia Gazette. "Burned At The Stake." August 11, 1905.

Bibliography

Evening Democrat. "Burned at the Stake." July 8, 1893.
Fisherman & Farmer. "Burned at the Stake." November 1, 1895.
Flake's Semi-Weekly Galveston Bulletin. "Mobb Murder." October 31, 1868.
Fort Wayne News. "Recalls A Horror." December 13, 1898.
Fort Wayne Sentinel. "Without Warrant of Law." September 26, 1906.
Fort Worth Gazette. "Still After Coy." February 19, 1892.
_____. "To Stop Lynching." January 16, 1893.
_____. "A Horrible Crime." January 28, 1893.
_____. "Hunting Smith." January 31, 1893.
_____. "Smith Caught." February 1, 1893.
_____. "Branded, Blistered, Burned." February 2, 1893.
_____. "It Was Just." February 3, 1893.
_____. "The Cause of the Trouble." February 6, 1893.
_____. "A Negro Mob." February 6, 1893.
_____. "Lynch Law." February 8, 1893.
_____. "The Higher Law." February 8, 1893.
_____. "That Message." February 9, 1893.
_____. "Maxey's View of It." February 11, 1893.
_____. "Texas Siftings." February 11, 1893.
_____. "Fannin Citizens." February 11, 1893.
_____. "Talk of Lynching." March 27, 1893.
_____. "No Lynching." April 2, 1893.
_____. "Inciting Violence." April 4, 1893.
_____. "Burrows." October 20, 1895.
_____. "Dark Spot." November 1, 1895.
Fort Worth Record. "Enraged Citizens Burn Negro Slayer." January 21, 1919.
Fort Worth Star-Telegram. "Enraged Citizens Dance Around Funeral Pyre as Three Negroes Pay Penalty for Girl's Death." May 7, 1922.
_____. "Negro Uprising Feared." May 8, 1922.
_____. "15 Arrested As Probe of Lynching Begins." May 10, 1922.
_____. "Sherman Put under Martial Law." May 11, 1930.
_____. "The Real Victims at Sherman." May 11, 1930.
_____. "Military Probe of Mob Acts Begun." May 12, 1930.
_____. "Negro Warnings Found at Sherman." May 13, 1930.
Galveston Daily News. "Barbarity." January 21, 1876.
_____. "Lawlessness—Barbarism—Radicalism." January 22, 1876.
_____. "Torch and Faggot." January 27, 1876.
_____. "Negro Burned at the Stake." December 29, 1885.
_____. "An Awful Expiation." October 27, 1891.
_____. "She Applied the Match." February 21, 1892.
_____. "Back from Detroit." February 22, 1892.
_____. "A Year of Revolting Crimes." August 3, 1892.
_____. "The Paris Horror." January 29, 1893.
_____. "The Rape Fiend Caught." February 1, 1893.
_____. "Myrtle Vance Murder." February 1, 1893.
_____. "Governor Hogg's Action." February 3, 1893.
_____. "Justified at Denison." February 4, 1893.
_____. "Hogg's Special Message." February 16, 1893.
_____. "The Atavism of Bestiality." August 6, 1893.
_____. "Judge Lynch A Felon." August 26, 1894.

_____. "Slowly Roasted." October 30, 1895.
_____. "To Have Trial Today." October 17, 1902.
_____. "Hanged Till Dead." October 18, 1902.
_____. "Majors Lynched." August 9, 1905.
_____. "Hanged and Burned." August 12, 1905.
_____. "Condemned Negro Taken from Jail and Burned." Jan. 21, 1919.
_____. "Indictment Flays Klan in Outrages." April 14, 1928.
_____. "Negro Rushed Out of Town after Attack by Citizens." December 9, 1933.
Glanton, Dahleen. "Running North: A Family History." *Chicago Tribune*, February 12, 1998.
Goshen Daily News. "Barbarism." February 2, 1893.
Granbury News. "Negro Meets Death at Stake in Tyler." October 30, 1912.
Greensboro Daily News. "Mexico Files Claim." November 10, 1910.
Hale, William T. "Matters and Things." *Alton Evening Telegraph*, October 20, 1906.
Hamer, Frank A. "Letter to Governor Dan Moody." May 13, 1930.
Harrisburg Telegraph. "Texas Mob Burns at Stake Negro Murderer of Woman." June 21, 1910.
Haskell News. "Angry Mob Burns Texas Negro." August 12, 1915.
Helper, Hinton Rowan. *The Impending Crisis of the South: How to Meet It*. New York: Burdick Brothers, 1857.
Hillsboro Mirror. "Bragg Williams Was Sentenced." January 22, 1919.
_____. "Negro Burned on Public Square" January 22, 1919.
_____. "Charge Given by Judge Horton B. Porter." January 29, 1919.
Honey Grove Signal. "Thoughts on the Race Question and the Fight." July 29, 1910.
_____. "Negroes Burned at Sulphur Springs." September 3, 1915.
Hopkinsville Kentuckian. "Negro Burned." August 15, 1905.
Houston Daily Post. "The Burning Question." September 7, 1901.
_____. "Negro Burned at the Stake." May 23, 1902.
_____. "Troops Ordered Out." October 16, 1902.
Houston Informer. "America's Reign of Lynch Law." July 10, 1920.
_____. "Officer, Waco's At It Again!" January 27, 1923.
Houston Post. "The Burning at the Stake." September 6, 1901.
_____. "The Tragedies." January 1, 1910.
_____. "Burning an Offender." October 22, 1921.
_____. "Texas Gallows Claims Last of Legal Victims." September 23, 1923.
_____. "East Texas Mob Cuts Heart Out of Slain Negro, Burns Body." December 9, 1933.
Humboldt Union. "No Indicements for Rodriguez Mob." December 24, 1910.
Ifill, Sherrilyn A. *On the Courthouse Lawn*. Boston: Beacon Press, 2007.
Ihejirika, Maudlyne. "Great Migration image is face of 'shock and terror.'" *Chicago Sun-Times*. September 17, 1910.
Indianapolis News. "Evans Is Witness as Klan Litigation Ends." April 13, 1928.
Iowa City Press-Citizen. "Mexican Is Burned at Stake." November 5, 1910.
James, P.L. *The facts in the case of the horrible murder of little Myrtle Vance and its fearful expiation at Paris, Texas, February 1st, 1893*.
Jarrett, Vernon. "An Old Photo Comes to Life." *Chicago Tribune*, February 10, 1980.
Jett, Brandon T. (2012). "The Bloody Red River: Lynching and Racial Violence in Northeast Texas, 1890-1930." Master's Thesis, Texas State University-San Marcos.
Kansas City Sun. "Waco Horror Stirs to Action." July 8, 1916.

Bibliography

Keowee Courier. "Negro Rapist Burned." June 4, 1902.
Lancaster Herald. "Axman Slays Three Children at Temple." August 6, 1915.
Laredo Weekly Times. "Burned Negro for Hammer Murders." August 1, 1915.
Lead Daily Call. "Body of Negro Is Burned by Mob in Texas." December 8, 1933.
Leavenworth Times. "Negro Burned at the Stake by Texas Mob." May 23, 1902.
Liberty Vindicator. "Burning Threatened." March 15, 1901.
_____. "Burned at Stake." June 24, 1910.
Liberator. "London Anti-Slavery Advocate." August 24, 1860.
Logansport Pharos-Tribune. "Negro Slayer of Officer Burned." May 20, 1922.
Longview News-Journal. "Family of Minister Who Set Himself on Fire Explains His Final Act." July 3, 2014.
Los Angeles Herald. "Sectional Bigotry and the Vance Incident." February 5, 1893.
_____. "Young Negro Is Burned at Stake." July 29, 1908.
Lowell Sun. "Burned at Stake." March 8, 1909.
Lubbock Morning-Avalanche. "Assaulter's Body Is Dragged Over Town By Crowds." May 10, 1930.
McDonald, Bobby. *Out of the Darkness: The Black Face of Hopkins County*. Sulphur Springs: Flippin Printing, 2002.
Meridian Tribune. "Burned A Black." October 5, 1900.
_____. "Mob Burns Two Negroes at Paris." July 9, 1920.
Morning Post. "Burned at the Stake." August 12, 1905.
Morning Times. "W. H. Vance Is Dead." December 13, 1898.
N.A.A.C.P. "The Burning of Bragg Williams." June 1919.
Naples Monitor. "Waco Negro Convicted of Murder by Jury Out Four Minutes." March 30, 1923.
Naugatuck Daily News. "Death of a Texan." December 13, 1898.
Navarro County Historical Society. *Navarro County History*. Quanah: Nortex Press, 1975.
Neville, Alexander W. *Paris News*. "Backward Glances." February 2, 1953.
_____. "Backward Glances: Pitt McGrew Was Terror to His Race in Paris." February 9, 1954
_____. "Backward Glances." February 21, 1955.
_____. "Backward Glances." February 2, 1956.
_____. "Backward Glances." November 11, 1956.
_____. "Backward Glances." May 17, 1968.
New York Age. "Texas Barbarians Lynch and Burn Another Man." June 13, 1912.
_____. "How Arthur Boys Were Lynched and Three Sisters Raped." September 4, 1920.
_____. "Texas Lynch Mob Cuts Out Heart of Victim Before Burning Him." December 16, 1933.
New York Call. "Sheriff Holds 2 Whites in Crime that 3 Burned For." May 7, 1922.
New York Times. "A Fiendish Revenge." October 14, 1883.
_____. "Burned at the Stake." October 27, 1891.
_____. "Another Negro Burned." February 2, 1893.
_____. "Gov. Hogg Aroused." February 3, 1893.
_____. "Negro Burned at the Stake." March 14, 1901.
_____. "Texas Negro Burned at Stake." August 21, 1901.
_____. "Lynching A Savage Relic." June 28, 1903.
_____. "Texas Mob Burns Negro at the Stake." September 8, 1905.
_____. "Negro Burned at the Stake." July 29, 1908.

_____. "Negro Burned at Stake." July 23, 1910.
_____. "2,000 Aid in Burning Negro at the Stake." May 26, 1912.
_____. "Two Negroes, One Dead, Burned at the Stake." August 30, 1915.
_____. "15,000 Witness Lynching." May 16, 1916.
_____. "Burn 2 Negroes at the Stake." July 7, 1920.
_____. "Texas Mob Burns Negro at the Stake." October 12, 1921.
_____. "Mob Burns Three Negroes at Stake." May 7, 1922.
_____. "Fresh Outrage in Waco at Grisly Lynching of 1916." May 1, 2005.
New York Tribune. "Negro Burned at Stake." September 8, 1905.
Newark Advocate. "Negro Burned at Stake for Murders." July 31, 1915.
Nocona News. "Negro Burned at the Stake." March 11, 1909.
Nolan County News. "Frenzied Crowd Mutilates and Burns Negro's Body." December 14, 1933.
Oakland Tribune. "Negro Burned at Stake." March 13, 1901.
Ocala Evening Star. "Negro Burned in Texas." September 8, 1905.
Oelwein Daily Register. "Negro Burned at Stake." June 22, 1910.
Orange Leader. "Heavy Guard Put Around Kountze Jail." December 8, 1933.
Ottawa Journal. "Negro Burnt at the Stake." March 8, 1909.
Palacios Beacon. "Negro Burned at The Stake." December 7, 1917.
Palestine Daily Herald. "Reward for Majors." July 18, 1905.
_____. "Was a Prey of the Flames." August 12, 1905.
_____. "Attempted Criminal Assault Happened Outside of Town." August 14, 1905.
_____. "Negro Burned at Stake." September 9, 1905.
_____. "Boiler Blew Up." March 22, 1906.
_____. "Burned at the Stake." March 8, 1909.
_____. "A Rapist Is Burned." June 21, 1910.
_____. "She Knew Her Well." June 24, 1910.
_____. "Burned at the Stake." November 4, 1910.
_____. "Grand Jury Investigating." December 15, 1910.
Paris Morning News. "Confession in Fryar Case Is Announced." May 11, 1916.
_____. "Investigation of Hillsboro Mob Has Started in Austin." January 24, 1919.
_____. "No Action Yet on Contempt Plea." February 22, 1919.
Paris News. "Mob Violence Flares Over Texas Attack; Jail Guarded." December 8, 1933.
_____. "Oldest Working Editor in Texas." July 14, 1970.
_____. "Arthur Lynchings in Paris Were 87 Years Ago." July 6, 2007.
Pella Herald. "The Work of Fiends." February 17, 1893.
Pittsburg Daily Headlight. "O. P. Bailey." June 12, 1901.
Plano Star-Courier. "Negro is Burned By Leesburg Mob." October 14, 1921.
Port Arthur News. "Negro Burned by Texas Mob." October 11, 1921.
_____. "Body of Negro Burned at Waco." May 27, 1922.
Post-Standard. "Negro Burned at Stake." March 14, 1901.
Progress-Examiner. "A negro who outraged." August 29, 1901.
Rabe, Elizabeth R. "African American Doughboys: Victory in France, Defeat in Dallas." *The Texas Historian.* Vol. 58, No. 1, September 1997.
Renwick Times. "Burned at the Stake." May 30, 1922.
Rochester Daily Republican. "Barbarism." February 2, 1893.
Rockwall County Herald-Banner. "Our Legacy of Shame." December 8, 2006.
Rusk Cherokeean. "Ed Kirkland, Negro." November 4, 1921.
Salt Lake Herald. "Negro Is Burned in Texas for the Murder of a White Woman."

Bibliography

August 21, 1901.
Salt Lake Herald-Republican. "Frenzied Men and Boys Apply Torch." July 23, 1910.
Salt Lake Tribune. "Burned At The Stake." September 29, 1902.
San Antonio Evening News. "Protest Against Lynching Is Filed." July 9, 1920.
San Antonio Express. "Prefers Jail to Freedom." June 15, 1912.
_____. "Swift Vengeance Taken." August 30, 1915.
_____. "Negro Who Attacked White Woman Is Burned At The Stake." December 7, 1917.
_____. "The Hill County Murderers." January 22, 1919.
_____. "Will Recommend New Legislation in His Message." January 22, 1919.
_____. "Steps to End Mob Rule in Texas Advocated in Legislature." January 23, 1919.
_____. "$1,000 Reward." January 24, 1919.
_____. "The Hillsboro Atrocity Investigated." January 25, 1919.
_____. "Mob Law Condemned." February 4, 1919.
_____. "Posses Seeking Negro Slayers of Farmer and Son." July 3, 1920.
_____. "Clue to Negro Slayer Traced." December 7, 1933.
San Antonio Light. "Cut Out Heart." October 26, 1972.
San Marcos Free Press. "Why Judge Lynch?" July 26, 1883.
San Saba Weekly News. "Cremated." November 6, 1891.
San Saba County News. "Horror of Horrors." February 10, 1893.
Santa Cruz Evening News. "Convicted Negro Burned by Texas Mob." January 20, 1919.
Sedalia Democrat. "Body of Negro Slain by Posse Burned in Texas." December 8, 1933.
Semi-Weekly Courier-Times. "Horrible Crime Committed in Cherokee County. June 25, 1910.
Semi-Weekly Farm Reporter. "Anderson Ellis Burned to Death." March 8, 1909.
Semi-Weekly Light. "Young Negro Burned Today." May 16, 1916.
Sherman Daily Democrat. "Lamar County Mob Burns Two Negroes for Double Murder." July 7, 1920.
_____. "Two Negroes Pay Penalty of Crime by Being Burned When Taken by Angry Mob." May 21, 1922.
Shiner Gazette. "A Negro Mob." November 23, 1893.
_____. "A Couple of Fakirs." December 21, 1893.
_____. "Negro Burned." June 1, 1922.
Sioux County Herald. "Burned at the Stake." May 28, 1902.
Smallwood, James. *Born in Dixie: The History of Smith County, Texas.* Austin: Eakin Press, 1998 (2 Vols).
Snyder Signal. "Negro Burned at Stake." May 31, 1912.
Southern Mercury. "Henry Smith, the Negro Fiend." February 9, 1893.
_____. "National Negro Council." August 5, 1897.
_____. "Murder and Outrage." August 22, 1901.
_____. "Fixed for a Barbecue." October 16, 1902.
_____. "Will Pay Reward." August 17, 1905.
_____. "A Negro Rapist Burned at Stake." August 17, 1905.
Springfield Missouri Republican. "To Try Nine on Charges of Lynching." December 5, 1922.
State Herald. "Tried And Hanged The Same Day." October 24, 1902.
_____. "A Negro Was Burned." October 3, 1902.
_____. "The Negro Who Assaulted Mrs. Norris." September 14, 1905.
_____. "Does The Future Give Hope?" September 14, 1905.

Steubenville Herald. "Race Riots in Texas Are Feared." July 8, 1920.
Sulphur Springs Gazette. "A Day of Tragedies and Horror." August 29, 1915.
Sunday Gazeteer. "Horrible." January 29, 1893.
_____. "Horror of Horrors." February 5, 1893.
Sweetwater Daily Reporter. "Guard Troops Ordered There." May 9, 1930.
Taylor County News. "The Law's Delay." November 20, 1891.
_____. "The Fearful Retribution." February 10, 1893.
_____. "A Negro Was Burned." July 14, 1893.
_____. "Public Sentiment." June 3, 1898.
_____. "Paris Is Quiet Following Big Negro Lynching." July 7, 1920.
Taylor Press. "Members of a Mob at Texarkana." May 26, 1922.
Temple Daily Telegram. "The Gentry Family." July 22, 1910.
_____. "Brutal Black Murderer Is Burned at the Stake." July 31, 1915.
_____. "Genesis of the Mob." July 31, 1915.
_____. "Lynching in Bell County Five Years Ago Recalled." July 31, 1915.
_____. "Victims of Negro Attacker Still in Grave Condition." July 31, 1915.
_____. "Web Tightens Around White Man in the Grimes Murder." August 1, 1915.
_____. "Will Reward Now Be Paid? Is Asked." August 1, 1915.
_____. "Grimes Murder Is Closed Incident, Declares Sheriff." August 2, 1915.
_____. "The Texas Press." August 3, 1915.
_____. "White Man Theory Is Not Abandoned." August 4, 1915.
_____. "Officers Have Not Examined Clothes." August 6, 1915.
_____. "Career of Will Stanley Traced Back to Abilene." August 8, 1915.
_____. "The Parson." August 9, 1915.
_____. "Injured Man Able To Be On Streets." August 10, 1915.
_____. "Negro Admits He Murdered Woman." May 10, 1916.
_____. "Negro Hanged By Tennessee Mob." April 23, 1918.
_____. "Negroes Peeved at Mob at Hillsboro." January 23, 1919.
_____. "Vindicates the Rangers." January 23, 1919.
_____. "Rangers Will Not Be Sent to Scene of Mob Violence." May 9, 1922.
_____. "Negro Youth Is Burned at Stake By Angry Mobs." May 19, 1922.
_____. "Negro Burned in Florida." December 9, 1922.
Texas Mesquiter. "Brief News Items from All Over Texas." October 14, 1921.
_____. "Riot Cases Are Sent to Austin." November 21, 1930.
_____. "Brick-Bats and Bouquets." March 1, 1935.
The Times (London). "Negro Burned at the Stake." March 9, 1909.
The Times (Philadelphia). "Startling Mastery of Lynch Law." February 3, 1893.
Times-Picayne. "Rape and Murder and the Penalty." September 12, 1861.
Tyler, George. W. *The History of Bell County*. San Antonio: The Naylor Company, 1936.
Tyler Morning Telegraph. "Madman of Martyr? Retired Minister Sets Self on Fire, Dies." July 1, 2014.
Vernon Record. "Legal Delay and Mob Law." January 24, 1919.
Waco Citizen. "Roy Mitchell Hanging Recalled in Dallas News." July 26, 1977.
Waco Evening News. "Hogg's Telegrams to the Paris Officials." February 4, 1893.
_____. "Against Lynch Law." February 13, 1893.
_____. "Gratified Vengeance." August 12, 1893.
Waco Morning News. "Temple Suspects Not Brought Here." August 1, 1915.
_____. "Where the Blame Lies." August 3, 1915.
_____. "Mrs. Lucy Fryar." May 10, 1916.

Bibliography

Waco News-Tribune. "Story of Tragedy." January 17, 1919.
_____. "Negro Laughs As Jury Gives Death Sentence." January 18, 1919.
_____. "Hillsboro Mob Burns Negro at City's Square." January 21, 1919.
_____. "Texas Negroes Lynched by Mobs After Assaults." May 21, 1922.
_____. "Texarkana Murder Cases Continued to December 14." Dec. 6, 1922.
_____. "Judge Castigates Ku Klux Klan in Blistering Terms." April 14, 1928.
_____. "Mob Mutilates Body of Negro at Kountze." December 9, 1933.
Washington Post. "Burned at the Stake." August 12, 1905.
_____. "2,000 See A Man Burned." May 26, 1912.
_____. "Mob Fails to Find Negro." May 27, 1912.
_____. "Two Negroes Lynched for Alleged Assaults." May 21, 1922.
_____. "A Texas Minister Sets Himself on Fire and Died to 'Inspire' Justice." July 16, 2014.
Washington Times. "Rangers Prepare to Fight Mexicans." November 12, 1910.
Waxahachie Daily Light. "Negro Burned at the Stake." August 11, 1905.
_____. "Our Ellis County Citizens Protect Their Homes." September 8, 1905.
_____. "One Hundred Lashes." September 13, 1905.
_____. "Negro Assaults Young Woman." July 28, 1908.
_____. "Negro Burned on the Square." July 29, 1908.
_____. "Fiend in Black Burned at Stake." May 5, 1912.
_____. "14 Indicted Sherman Men Are in Jail." May 21, 1930.
_____. "91 Truebills Returned by Grand Jury." May 29, 1930.
_____. "Sherman Riot Suspects Trial Is Postponed." June 23, 1930.
Weatherford Enquirer. "The Majesty of the Law." November 12, 1891.
_____. "Lynch Law." May 12, 1892.
Weekly Democrat-Gazette. "Burned Up Is the Black Fiend." July 30, 1908.
_____. "Camp County Negro Burned At The Stake." Oct. 13, 1921.
Weekly Herald. "Sulphur Springs Mob Burns Two Negroes." September 2, 1915.
Weekly Telegraph. "Texas Items." September 18, 1861.
Wells-Barnett, Ida B. *On Lynchings*. New York: Humanity Books, 2002.
West Texas News. "Burned At The Stake." July 31, 1908.
Whiteright Sun. "Mob Burns Two Negroes." August 30, 1915.
_____. "Sherman Riot Cases Are Dismissed." June 9, 1932.
Wichita Beacon. "Negro Is Burned." March 13, 1901.
Wichita Daily Eagle. "The Burning of Negroes and Its Causes." September 30, 1893.
Wichita Daily Times. "Seventh and Eighth Lynchings for May Staged on Saturday." May 21, 1922.
Wills Point Chronicle. "Burned at the Stake." October 31, 1895.
The World. "Paris Citizens Proud of It." February 3, 1893.
York Daily. "Clash Eminent of Texas Border." November 16, 1910.

Index

1910 Slocum Massacre: An Act of Genocide in East Texas, The 161, 191

A

Abilene Reporter 36, 124
Abilene Reporter-News 36
Abilene, Texas 22, 36, 124, 166, 176
Aitch, J. W. 142
Akers, Monte 121, 125
Akers, Sheriff 102-103
Alabama Landing, Texas 38, 158
Aldrich, J. W. 135
Allen, Roy 139, 141
Allison, Dr. W. L. 110
An Eye for An Eye or The Fiend and the Fagot: An Unvarnished Account of the Burning of Henry Smith at Paris, Texas, February 1, 1893, and the Reason he was Tortured 3, 32
Angleton, Texas 130
Antlers, Oklahoma 8
Arizona Republican 21, 166
Armor, Bill 160
Army of the Potomac 160
Arnold, Jimmie 139-141
Arthur, Ervin 113-116, 158
Arthur, Herman 113-116, 158
Arthur, Scott 113, 115-116
Arthur, Violet 113, 115-116
Athens, Texas 93
Atlanta Constitution 161, 166
Ausley, Eula 121, 125
Austin Statesman 23, 152
Austin, Texas 2, 14, 20-23, 30, 77, 135, 140, 148, 150, 152, 158, 166, 168, 174-176

B

Bagwell Station, Texas 9-10
Bagwell, Texas 5, 9-10
Bailey, Fred Arthur 92
Bailey, O.P. 33
Baker, Sheriff J. W. 54
Baker, John M. 40
Baldwin, W. S., M. D 5
Balmer and Weber Music House Company 24
Balmer, Charles 24
Bane, W. F. 85, 168
Bardwell Evening Democrat 32
Bardwell, Kentucky 32
Barnum & Baily 52
Barrow, Clyde 164
Beaumont Journal 144, 146, 167
Beckville, Texas 63
Bell County, Texas 40, 55, 88, 90, 95-96, 100-101, 176
Bell, Leonard 52
Bell, Mrs. Leonard 49-50, 53
Belton, Texas 88-90, 96, 158
Bennett College 161
Berry, E. A. 111
Bexar County, Texas 77, 94
Black, James H. 159
Blooming Grove, Texas 70
Bloomington, Texas 132
Blossom, Texas 4-5
Bolton, Harold 128, 130
Bonds, Albert 96
Bonham, Texas 13
Born In Dixie: The History of Smith County, Texas 94, 163
Boston Daily Globe 20, 167

178

Index

Boston, Massachusetts 164
Boston Post 20, 167
Boyd, Judge Ben W. 141
Bradford, Capt. 39
Bragg, Natural 110
Brazoria County, Texas 130
Brazos River 68
Breckenridge Daily American 118, 167
Brenham Daily Banner 65, 167
Briggs, C. E. 139, 141
Broaddus, Andrew Sidney 41, 160
Brockman, Nellie Williams 142-143, 147
Brooks, Allen 87
Brooks, Clem 9
Brown, Jordan 72
Brownwood Bulletin 123, 130, 167
Brownwood Daily Bulletin 84, 168
Brownwood News 101
Bryan Daily Eagle and Pilot 94, 167
Buchanan, Jim 65-66
Buchanan, Texas 153
Buenger, Walter L. 34
Buford Park 102-103, 158
Burch, Henry 92
Burkes, David C. 88
Burleson County, Texas 161
Burns, Jarrett 160
Burton, Marvin "Red" 128
Butler, Roy 163
Butler, Sheriff J. B. 101-103, 162-163
Butler, William 7-8, 29
Buzbee, Daniel Washington Harris 36

C

Caddo Creek 78
Caddo Mills, Texas 83
Cady, J. D. 67
Caldwell, Clifford R. 162-163
Caldwell, J. M. 59, 161
Caldwell, Mrs. J. M. 59-60
Cameron Herald 95, 167
Cameron, Texas 40-41, 95, 158, 167
Campbell, Governor Thomas 91, 163
Camp County, Texas 118, 120, 158, 167, 177
Canonsburg Weekly Notes 26, 167
Carlisle, J. A. 140
Carter, Judge R. M. 136, 139
Carthage, Texas 63
Cass County, Texas 44-46, 158-159, 167
Cate, Alexander 2, 5, 7-8, 10-12, 14
Celeste, Texas 83
Centreville Conservative 38
Cessna, G. K. 38
Chance, Ralph B. 143
Chaney, Wilbur 68
Chapman, J. B., M.D. 5
Cherokee County, Texas 86, 158, 175
Cherry, Jim 69, 161
Chicago Daily Globe 24
Chicago Defender 116
Chicago History Museum 116
Chicago, Illinois 115-116
Chicago Tribune 114-115, 172
Chicago Urban League 116
Chickasaw Nation 59
Choate, Dick 126
Civil War 38, 67, 121, 156, 160, 166
Clark, Andrew 82-83
Clarkson, William Everett "Eb" 115
Clarksville, Texas 5, 9, 22
Cleburne, Texas 22, 153
Cleveland Daily Leader 153, 167
Clinton, Texas 78
Clow, Arkansas 6-7, 10
"Cocoanut, Jack" 150-152, 158, 164
Coke, Governor Richard 41
Cole, Leslie 139, 141
Collins, Walter 108, 110
Colorado City, Texas 80
Comanche County, Texas 46
Comanche, Texas 46
Conditt, Herschell 76
Conditt, Jesse 76
Conditt, Joseph 76
Conditt, Lora 76
Conroe, Texas 126-127, 158, 168
Cooke County, Texas 60, 140-141
Coolidge, Texas 118

Cooper, Judge R. L. 97
Corbin, Gran 68
Cornish, Johnnie 122, 124-125, 131, 156, 158
Corsicana Daily Sun 145, 168
Corsicana, Texas 54, 158
Cowin, Daniel 11
Cox, Joe 135
Coy, Ed 9, 11, 47, 48, 158, 161
Crisis 127
Crockett Sentinel 38
Crook, G.M. 9, 159
Crook, J. Morgan 115
Cuero, Texas 77
Culp, William C. 140
Cureton, Calvin M. 111-112, 163
Curry, Snap 121-122, 124-125, 131, 158
Curtis, Judge A. L. 90

D

Dahomey 160
Dallas County, Texas 87, 105, 139-140
Dallas Express 109, 168
Dallas Morning News 3-4, 7, 20, 32, 48-49, 53, 60-61, 64, 67, 83, 88, 93, 99, 118, 131, 141, 150, 160, 162-163, 168, 170, 174, 176
Dallas Public Library 7, 55-58, 87
Dallas, Texas 3, 7, 13, 20, 22, 32, 48-49, 53-61, 64, 67, 74, 83, 87-88, 93, 99, 105, 108-109, 117-118, 131, 139-141, 150, 160, 162-163, 168, 170, 174, 176
Dallas Times-Herald 22, 54
Darfur, Sudan 157
Datura, Texas 118
Davis, C.A. 53
Davis, Dan 92-94, 158
Davis, Jesse 132-133, 158
Davis, Steve 53, 70-76, 92-94, 132-133, 158
De Kalb, Texas 5-6, 12
De La Barra, Francisco León 91, 162
Delancey, Mrs. 78
Delancey, R. H. 78

Delancey, Viola 78-80, 128
Delord, Ronald G. 162-63
Denison, Texas 13, 22-23, 59, 171
Denton, Ben H. 114
de Pontes, L. B. 54
Dernal, Texas 132, 158
Detroit, Texas 5, 171
DeWitt County, Texas 77
Dewitt, U. W. 115
Dexter, Texas 60
Díaz, President Porfirio 162
Dixon Evening Telegraph 1
Doak, N.P. 22
Dollins, John 105-106
Donaldsonville Chief 91, 170
Douglassville, Texas 44-46, 158
Dowery, Bob 8
Dugan, George B. 83

E

Eakin Press 1, 94, 163
Early, Junius M. 32-33
Edna, Texas 76
Edwards County, Texas 91, 158
Edwards, John 140-141
Ellis, Anderson 82-84, 158, 175
Ellis County, Texas 158
Ellis, Jacob A. 68
El Paso Herald 60, 94, 156, 170
Equal Justice Initiative 164
Eubank, George M. 85
Eubank, Jessie Shain 164
Eula, Ausley 121-122, 125
Evans, Dr. H. W. 117

F

Facts in the Case of the Horrible Murder of Little Myrtle Vance and its Fearful Expiation at Paris, Texas, February 1, 1893, The 6, 13, 16, 21, 32, 159
Fairview, Texas 122, 125
Fannin County, Texas 103
Farlow, Mrs. 134-135

Index

Farlow, Ned 134
Fate, Texas 82
Ferguson, Governor James E. 96
Ferguson State Farm 131
Field, Julien C. 23
Fishback, Governor William Meade 24
Flake's Semi-Weekly Bulletin 164
Flames After Midnight: Murder, Vengeance and the Desolation of a Texas Community 121, 125
Fleming, Sam S. 105
Flint, A. L. 96
Flippin, Nathan Asa 101-102, 163, 173
Fort Wayne Sentinel 78, 171
Fort Worth Daily Gazette 49, 52-53
Fort Worth Gazette 4, 18-19, 21-22, 29-31, 42, 171
Fort Worth Star-Telegram 134-135, 138, 139, 171
Fort Worth, Texas 4, 7, 13, 18-19, 21-22, 29, 31, 42, 49, 52, 55, 96, 110, 128, 134-135, 138-139, 171, 191
Frank Leslie's Illustrated Newspaper 45, 149
Frazier, A. M. 108, 110
Frazier, Dennis 85
Freestone County, Texas 121-122, 125, 158, 167
French, Homer 143
Fryar, George 104
Fryar, Lucy 104, 177
Fulton, Arkansas 6

G

Gaines, Ed 47
Gainesville Daily Hesperian 49, 53, 168
Galaway, Clement 44
Galveston Daily News 8, 15, 20, 22, 41, 45, 47, 49, 66, 68, 143, 171
Garcia, Arthur 165
Gay, George 131
Gentry, Henry 88-90, 158
Gibson, Monk 76-77
Gildersleeve, Fred 107
Goddess of Liberty 30

Grand Saline, Texas 148-149, 156, 164
Grantham, W. B. 55
Grayson County Courthouse 135, 141
Grayson County, Texas 24, 59-60, 134-135, 138-141, 158, 164, 170
Grayson, Florine 130-131
Greeley, Horace 165
"Green" 34-35, 158
Green, Lee 45-46, 159, 161
Greenville Morning Herald 86
Greenville, Texas 78-81, 83, 86, 156, 158, 166-168
Gregory, David 142-147, 158
Gregory, Mrs. 145
Griffin, General Charles 38-39, 160
Griggs, Nettie 68-69, 71
Grimes, Frank 96
Grimes, Marguerite 95-96
Grimes, Mary 95-97, 101
Grimes, William R. 95-96, 100
Grimes, Willie 95

H

Hallettsville, Texas 76
Hallsville, Texas 62-63, 65
Hamer, Frank 135-137, 164, 172
Hamilton, Will 140-141
Hammond, Deputy Sheriff 55
Hammond, D. S. 14
Hardin County, Texas 7, 143, 158
Hardy, Colonel G. W. 57
Harlem, New York 161
Harlem Renaissance 161
Harmon, Winnie 162-163
Harris, Claude J. 96
Harrison County, Texas 158
Harrison, Rodell "Slim" 96-99
Harris, Sam 128-130
Hayden, Bud 161
Haynie, Judge George R. 126
Hays, Maggie 128-130
Helper, Hinton Rowan 164-165
Hempstead County, Arkansas 10
Hemsell, David L. 79
Henderson, Jonas "John" 54-55, 158

Henderson, Mrs. Lem 90
Henderson, Texas 65
Hickory Creek 29
Hicks Family 65
Hicks, James T. 10-11
Hillard, Henry 49-53, 94, 158
Hillard, Robert 49
Hill County, Texas 108, 110-112, 168, 175
Hill, Ervin 113-116
Hillsboro, Texas 54-55, 108-111, 158, 168-169, 172, 174-177
History of Bell County, The 101, 176
History Press, The 161, 167
Hoar, Senator George Frisbie 27, 160
Hobbs, Phil 94
Hobby, Governor William P. 111
Hodges, J.C. 23
Hodges, J. H. 113-114
Hodges, Jim 162-163
Hodges, William 113-114
Hogg, Governor James 6, 14, 20-24, 27-29, 33, 45-46, 159-160, 166, 169, 171, 173, 176
Holman, H.B. 10
Honey Grove Signal 103, 162, 172
Honey Grove, Texas 103, 134, 162, 172
Hope, Arkansas 11
Hopkins County, Texas 69, 101-102, 173
Houston Chronicle 124, 145
Houston Informer 113, 172
Houston Post 54, 64, 82, 118, 132, 172
Howard, Texas 70
Hubbard, William 165
Hughes, George 134, 137-139, 158
Humphrey, William 42
Humphries, Judge J. A. 97
Hunt County, Texas 78-80, 83, 102
Hunt, J.C. 5

I

Impending Crisis of the South: How to Meet It 164-165, 172
Indianapolis Sentinel, The 25
International Center of Photography 11
Italy, Texas 71

J

James, P.L. 32
Jefferson County, Texas 143
Jefferson, Texas 63
Jenkins, Dr. F. H. 71
Jenkins, Lee 129
Jewell, Henry W. 47
Jewell, Julia 47-48
Jim Crow 113, 132, 156
Johnson, Albert 74
Johnson, Carrie 92-94
Johnson, Leonard 86-87, 158
Johnson, Louis 161
Johnson, Mary 85
Johnson, Sank 129
Joiner, John 42, 158
Jones, Jeff (Slim) 139, 141
Jones, Mose 122, 124-125, 131, 158
Jordan, Sheriff Miles D. 143-146

K

Katy Railroad 68
Katy, Texas 128
Kaufman County, Texas 158
Keeling, W. A. 111-112
Kerens, Texas 42, 158
Khmer Rouge 157
Kilgore, Texas 50, 63
King, Irene 118
King, Jim 49, 53
King, Otis 122
Kiomatia River 8
Kirven, Texas 121-123, 125, 156, 158, 168
Kountze, Texas 142-143, 145-147, 158, 167, 174, 177
Ku Klux Klan 117, 167, 177

L

Lake Charles, Louisiana 162
Lake Waxahachie 70
Lamar County 4-5, 10-11, 14-15, 21-22, 30, 36, 114-115, 158-160, 164, 175
Lamb, Mrs. 88
Lancaster Herald 95, 173

Index

Lanham, Governor Samuel W. T. 77
Lanier, Isaac H. 45-46
Lansing Switch 62-65
Las Vacas, Mexico 90
Lee, Nathan 130
Leesburg, Texas 118, 120, 158, 174
Lenoir Topic 24
Leon County, Texas 38, 158
Leonidas, Texas 126
Lewis, Jerry 69
Liberator, The 164
Library of Congress 6, 13, 16, 21, 50-51, 53, 105-107
Limestone County, Texas 158
Linden Alliance Standard 45-46, 161, 166
Linden, Texas 45, 161
Little River 96
London Times 44
Lone Star, Texas 86-87, 158
Long. J. R. G. 28-29
Longview News-Journal 150, 173
Longview, Texas 62-63, 65, 150, 173
Los Angeles Herald 21, 25, 173
Lowe, John 44
Lowe, Mrs. 44
Lucas, Dr. W. W. 115
Ludlow, Clarence W. 117
Lummus, A. J. 126

M

Madero, Fransico I. 162
Majors, Sank 67-68, 168, 172, 174
Mansfield, Texas 76
Marshall Evening Messenger 20, 49
Marshall, Texas 20, 22, 34-35, 49, 62-63, 65, 96, 158, 161, 163, 170
Marsh, R. H. 32
Mart Herald 101
May, Jim 139, 141
Mayo, Horace 121, 131
McCasland, J. B. 139-140
McCauley, Albert 85
McClure, E. L. 129
McCoy, J. E. 135
McCuistion, E.A. 14, 20, 160

McCuistion, Margaret 36, 37, 160
McCuistion, Mitchell Henderson 36
McCurtain County, Oklahoma 115
McDuffy, Smithy 110
McGelsey, J. Markus 162
McGrew, Pitt 114, 173
McKee, J. W. 62, 64
McKee, Mrs. J. W. 62, 64-65
McKinney, Arthur 82, 84
McKinney Democrat 42, 49, 69
McKinney, Mrs. 82
McKinney, Texas 42, 49, 69, 80, 82, 84-85, 119, 162-163
McKinney Weekly Democrat-Gazette 80, 119, 177
McLellan, James 35
McLellan, Martha 34
McLennan County, Texas 54, 67, 94, 104, 105, 128, 130
McNamara, John B. 105
McNeel, Tom 46
McNeely, Wylie 118-120, 158
Medicine Lodge, Kansas 41
Metropolitan Museum of Art. The 154
Mexia, Texas 58
Mexican Revolution 91
Milam County, Texas 40, 158
Mildred, Conditt 76
Milford, Texas 71
Miller, Charles 32
Miller County, Arkansas 126
Minnick, Joe P. 70-72, 74
Mitchell, Jim 88
Mitchell, Roy 130
Mitchusson, William E. 40-41
Montgomery, Texas 32
Montrose, T. D. 79
Moody, Governor Dan 135, 137, 139, 172
Moore, Charles Robert 148-150
Moore, Hardy Goodner 114, 163
Morgan, Alvin 139-141
Morgan, Dudley 62-63, 158
Morning Post 69
Mount Pleasant, Texas 120
Mount Vernon, Texas 7, 62

Mud Creek 59
Munden, George W. 64
Munroe, R. L. 105-106

N

Nacogdoches County, Texas 65-66
National Association for the Advancement of Colored People 115, 127, 173
National Citizens' Rights Association 161
Navarro County Historical Society 58, 173
Navarro County History 58, 173
Navarro County, Texas 54-56, 58, 70, 158, 173
Naylor Company 101, 176
Nazi Germany 157
Nebraska State Journal 26
Neches River 162
Nelson, William Columbus 60
Neville, Alexander 13, 33, 36, 164
New Boston, Texas 6
New York Age 114, 173
New York Herald 23
New York, New York 20, 22-23, 62, 76, 114-115, 159, 161, 165, 172-174, 177
New York Public Library 161
New York Times 20, 22, 62, 76, 115, 173
Nibling, Albert 97
Nichols, Joseph F. 80
Nolan County News 146, 164, 174
No Resting Place 42
Norris, Mrs. S.P. 70-72, 76, 175
Norris, S. P. 70, 75
Northington, D. K. 100
Norwood, C. K. "Knox" 86-87

O

Offenhauser Park 126
Oldham, Major William 160
Oldham, Phillis 160
O'Neal, Leonard (Baldy) 139, 141
Orange Leader 145, 174
Orange, Texas 145
Overton, Texas 63

Owen, Huley 125-126, 158
Owens, Gibbert 10
Ozan, Arkansas 6, 10

P

Page, Dr. 164
Palestine Daily Herald 33, 36, 68, 82, 86, 174
Palmer, Texas 76
Paris Daily News 13, 22, 28, 29
Paris Horror, The 1, 3, 5, 7, 9, 11, 13, 15, 17, 19, 21, 23, 25, 27, 29, 31, 33, 169, 171
Paris News 115, 164, 173, 174
Paris, Texas 1-3, 5-17, 19-33, 36, 49, 53-54, 60, 78, 80, 95, 113-116, 152-153, 156, 158-160, 164, 166, 168-177
Parker, Bonnie 164
Parks, Constable Logan 96
Peeler, A. J. 41
Perry, Sid 151
Pine Island Bayou 143
Pippen, Judge Charles A. 140
Pittsburgh, Kansas 33
Pittsburgh, Pennsylvania 117
Pittsburg, Texas 63, 120
Plano Star-Courier 120, 174
Plessy v. Ferguson 48
Port Arthur News 120, 174
Porter, Horton B. 110-112, 172
Powell, Audrey 125
Powell, Claude 96, 125
Powell, Texas 92, 125
Price, George A. 94
Purdom, Webb 139, 141

R

Raleigh Morning Post 69, 173
Ransom, Ella 160
Ransom, John 160
Reconstruction 38-39, 156, 160, 163-164
Red Branch, Texas 59-60
Redden, Maude 86-87
Redden, W. H. 86

Index

Redding, Oscar 151-152
Red River 5, 8-9, 36, 60, 172
Red River County 5, 8-9
Red River Valley Then and Now, The 36
Reese, George 4
Reese, John J. 118, 120
Reinhard, Capt. 38-39
Reno, Texas 4
Reynolds, Horace 139, 141
Richardson, Clifton Frederick, Sr. 163
Richardson, Sheriff W. W. "Bill" 143
Richmond, Joe 101-103, 158, 163
Richmond, King 101-103, 158, 163
Roberts, H. G. 55, 57
Robertson, Naby 10
Robinson, James 10
Robinson, Judge John 90
Robinson, Wiley B. 55-56, 58
Robinson, William Sherod 40
Rockdale, Texas 33, 40
Rock Springs, Texas 90-91, 158
Rockwall County, Texas 83, 174
Rockwall, Texas 82, 158
Rodriquez, Antonio 90, 158
Rogers, J. V. 34
Rogers, Texas 96
Roper, Jess 139, 141
Royce City, Texas 82
"Rube" 36, 37, 158, 160
Runnels, Henry 32
Rusk County, Texas 65
Rusk, Texas 86
Ryan, John 87

S

San Antonio El Regidor 49
San Antonio Express 25, 143, 153, 162-163, 175
San Antonio Register 142, 166
San Antonio, Texas 25, 49, 94, 142-143, 153, 162-163, 165-166, 175, 176
San Francisco Bulletin 104
San Marcos Free Press 40, 175
Santa Fe Railroad 100

Savage, Judge H. B. 90
Sayers, Governor Joseph D. 54, 57, 59-60, 65
Schomburg, Arturo Alfonso "Arthur" 161
Schomburg Center for Research in Black Culture 161
Scurry, Thomas 57, 58
Seminole Territory 162
Shanklin, Jim 8, 12
Sheppard, Floyd 140-141
Sherman, Texas 7, 13, 134-140, 156, 158-159, 164, 167-171, 175, 177
Shiner Gazette 49, 175
Shipp, Bart 134
Silsbee, Texas 145
Simmons, John 140-141
Simpson, Judge R. W. 163
Simpson, Palmer 162
Smallwood, James 94
Smith, Anthony 40, 158
Smith, Constable 102
Smith County Courthouse 162
Smith County, Texas 50, 94, 162-163, 175
Smith, Dr. M. 68
Smith, Edward 165
Smith, Henry 1-25, 27-34, 40-41, 45, 49-50, 59, 68, 78-81, 83, 94, 96, 100, 102, 128, 152-153, 157-160, 162-166, 169-171, 175
Smith, Leila 28-29
Smith, Sheriff Hugh 52, 96, 100, 162-163
Smith, Sue 2, 28-29
Smith, Ted 78-81, 83, 128, 158
Smith, Wig 50, 52, 162
Sofey, Bill 139, 141
Southern Mercury 59, 65, 68-69, 175
Southwestern Historical Quarterly 34, 92, 167
Sparks, Sam 55
Spindler, Charles 165
Sprendel's Mill 6
Springfield Leader 21
Stanley, Will 95-96, 98-101, 158, 166, 169, 176
Stephens, Sallie 46

St. Louis, Missouri 24, 26
St. Louis Republic 26
Strange, John 126
Streetman, Texas 130-131
Sturgeon, B. B. 10-11, 164
Sulphur Springs Gazette 69, 102, 162, 176
Sulphur Springs, Texas 7, 22, 68-69, 101-103, 156, 158, 162, 168-169, 172-173, 176, 177

T

Taylor, J. H. 74
Tazewell, Texas 101
Teel, Alex 151, 152
Temple Daily Telegram 89-90, 97, 99-101, 176
Temple, Texas 95, 158
Terrell, Chester H. 163
Terrell, Texas 117, 158
Texarkana, Arkansas 47, 126
Texarkana, Texas 6-7, 9, 11-12, 63, 125-126, 156, 158
Texas and Pacific Railroad 4, 7, 11, 62
Texas Central Railroad 6
Texas Lawmen, 1900-1940: More of the Good and the Bad 162-163
Texas Rangers 56, 91, 108, 110, 135, 137-38, 176-177
Texas State Library & Archives Commission 79, 81
Texas State Lunatic Asylum 150
Thomas, Jesse 129-130, 158
Thompson, W. H. S. 117
Tilley, G. W. 67
Titus County, Texas 120
Tourgée, Albion Winegar 48, 161
Tucker, Rasho 85
Turner, Pete 40
Tyler Morning Telegraph 149-150, 176
Tyler, Texas 49, 51-53, 92-94, 95, 101, 149, 156, 158, 162-163, 169, 172, 176

U

United Methodist Church 148
U. S. State Department 91

V

Valiant, Oklahoma 114
Van Alstyne, Texas 139
Vance, Beuford D. 16-17, 159
Vance, Effie 159
Vance, Eugene 159
Vance, Henry 1-2, 6, 11, 16, 24, 32-33, 159
Vance, John C. 159
Vance, Myrtle 1-6, 11, 13, 16, 21-23, 27-28, 30, 32, 159, 169, 171-172
Vanoy, Jess 110
Vernon Record 108, 176
Victoria County, Texas 132, 158
Victoria, Texas 22, 132
Voth, Texas 143-144

W

Waco News-Tribune 108, 177
Waco, Texas 54, 58, 74, 93-94, 104-108, 121, 128-130, 156, 158, 166-168, 170, 172-174, 176, 177
Waco-Times Herald 121
Walker, Jack 160
Walker, Jim 161
Walters, B. 10
Washington, Arkansas 6, 10
Washington, D. C. 27, 53
Washington, Jesse 98, 104-105, 107, 158, 169
Washington Post 94, 150, 177
Waxahachie Daily Light 69-70, 72-76, 177
Waxahachie, Texas 69-74, 140, 177
Weatherford Weekly Herald 162-163
Wells, Annie 108, 110
Wells, Curtis 108
Wells, Dicey 96-99
Wells, George 108
West Texas News 80, 177
Wheatley, J. B. 135

White, J.L. 10
Whitesboro, Texas 59-61
Wildner, Abe 58-61, 158, 161, 166, 168
Wiley, Tom 70
Wilkerson Building 97, 99
Williams, Bragg 108-112, 158, 172-173
Williams, Tom 68-69, 158
Wills Point Chronicle 49, 177
Wilson, Lee 158, 161
Winn, Alex 118, 158
Winters, Joe 126-128, 158
Without Sanctuary: Lynching Photography in America 98
Wolfe, Cleo 139-141
Woods, J. E. Woods 131
Woods, Lewis 161
World War I 113
World War II 5, 164

Y

Younger, Conway 54, 56
Younger, Valley Dale 54

About the Author

Born in Fort Worth and raised in Aledo, Texas, E. R. Bills received a degree in journalism from Texas State University. He does freelance historical, editorial and travel writing for publications around the state and he is the author of *Texas Obscurities: Stories of the Peculiar, Exceptional and Nefarious* (History Press, 2013) and *The 1910 Slocum Massacre: An Act of Genocide in East Texas* (History Press, 2014), the latter of which led to a much-contested but successful effort to erect a state historical marker commemorating the victims of the Slocum Massacre.

www.ingramcontent.com/pod-product-compliance
Lightning Source LLC
Chambersburg PA
CBHW061308110426
42742CB00012BA/2099